Make Money Playing Video Games

The how to from start to finish

(Your Step By Step Guide To Making Money With Online Games)

John Hopper

Published By **Simon Dough**

John Hopper

Make Money Playing Video Games: The how to from start to finish (Your Step By Step Guide To Making Money With Online Games)

ISBN 978-1-77485-636-9

Legal & Disclaimer

The information contained in this ebook is not designed to replace or take the place of any form of medicine or professional medical advice. The information in this ebook has been provided for educational & entertainment purposes only.

The information contained in this book has been compiled from sources deemed reliable, and it is accurate to the best of the Author's knowledge; however, the Author cannot guarantee its accuracy and validity and cannot be held liable for any errors or omissions. Changes are periodically made to this book. You must consult your doctor or get professional medical advice before using any of the suggested remedies, techniques, or information in this book.

Table Of Contents

Introduction

As with any good book, it is important to start with an informative introduction.

This book will show how to start a YouTube Channel that allows you to earn a full-time income by playing videogames. This isn't all fun and games, even though it sounds very glamorous. While I will make this process as simple and painless as possible, it is not easy to become a star.

In reality, a gaming channel that is profitable is a serious business. This means it takes work just like any other business. We are going to look at this from a business point of view, as it is how you will distinguish yourself from the serious channels and those that get ignored.

I've worked with YouTubers like you that started out small and went on to earn a living producing gaming videos. YouTube has made this all possible. There's no reason you shouldn't want to be the next YouTuber.

Once you are ready, you can move on to the first chapter. Any business is successful if it has a plan.

Choosing Your Niche

A channel that focuses on one topic will help you build a fan base. It's essential to discover your niche.

This means your channel should first be focused on one particular game or group of games. This ensures that viewers of one video will also be interested to see the rest.

Let me use an example to illustrate.

If I had a channel dedicated to one game, anyone who visits the channel will be interested in it. They'd also be interested the other videos I have, as they're all related to that particular game. Because they are sure to find my content interesting, they are more likely and likely to sign up for my channel.

On the other side, let's pretend that my channel doesn't have a niche.

If I upload one video of myself playing a game of first-person gunner and the next I start uploading videos where I play a music game, the chances are that the person who is interested in first-person shooter won't be interested either in the game or vice versa. They won't bother subscribing to my channel, as it isn't relevant.

It's easier to retain viewers if you focus on a single niche. This will increase your chances of keeping them watching your videos over and over again.

This doesn't mean that you can't try new things later. You'll probably eventually want more fans so you can branch out! It is crucial that you keep your viewers in the beginning. It is difficult at first to find new viewers so you want them to stay.

Gaming Videos of All Types

After choosing your niche, you can then start to plan the types of videos you will make.

Let's go over some of the most popular types of gaming videos so you can decide which one would suit you best.

Commentaries (also known "Let's Play") are also called videos.

Commentaries are one of the most common types of gaming videos uploaded to YouTube. Commentaries show the user playing through a videogame, giving feedback and sharing their thoughts. These videos can be made quickly because there is very little preparation and minimal editing.

Unfortunately, YouTube has the highest number of them, which means they are difficult to get noticed. Viewers seeking commentary videos do so for entertainment purposes. To stand out among your competitors, you must be more entertaining than theirs. This can be done by being light-hearted and humorous.

I strongly recommend that you analyze the comments of your favourite commentators, and take inspiration from their strategies. While creating your own approach to your commentary, it is also a good idea. You want entertainment, but most importantly, you want something unique.

Commentaries make you, the person, more important than what is happening in the game. Do not forget that!

Tutorials

Tutorial videos offer a complete alternative to commentaries. Tutorial videos serve a purpose other than entertainment. It might be to achieve a certain level in the game. Perhaps it's the fastest way for a boss to be killed. Maybe it's to achieve a goal. Whatever the purpose, they want to know how to do something.

These videos are much more difficult to produce because not only do you need to show the viewer how it is done, but you also need to be able and clear to explain how it is done. They should be easily able to reproduce what you're showing.

These videos are difficult to create and make it much easier for you to get your videos found.

Reviews

Gaming reviews have become incredibly popular. No one wants to waste their money when buying a brand new game. It's a great way to attract people to your videos, as they will start to play the games and be honest about their experience. They'll remember you and be more likely to watch your videos than anyone else because you are familiar with them.

Other

These three categories are a majority of YouTube gaming videos. However, there are plenty of other categories you could consider. Glitch videos, montage videos, "top 10" videos etc. People love to watch these solid videos.

You can analyze your viewing habits to find what you enjoy. If you love something, chances are that others will too. Give it to them and they will come back for more.

Defining Your Target Audience

This is where you really get into the business mode. Now is the time to research and identify your target audience. It is important to determine who you want to see your channel. This will enable you tailor your videos accordingly.

The business world has a saying that says "If you try to appeal all people, you'll end-up appealing to none." YouTube is no different. We'll take the time necessary to understand your target audience.

Think of your ideal audience. What is their average age? What is their gender? What are their marital and income statuses? How will these demographics influence their viewing habits

Which part is it? What is their preferred time online? This will enable you to establish a uploading schedule that ensures your videos reach the greatest number of people.

Which type of games do your ideal viewer prefer? Why does your ideal viewer like this particular type of game? How can you adapt your videos to appeal to their interests?

These are all very important. They affect who views your videos and how they view them. By being able to identify your viewer's preferences, you can provide the best content possible for them. And your audience will thank you for it.

This is the stuff that separates professionals from amateurs. I know you mean well, and would not have purchased this book if you didn't.

Choosing Your Channel Name

Now it's the time to actually create your channel. If you have not already registered an account on YouTube.com, click here. Read this section first.

We're currently choosing a name to your channel. You may not realize it, but the name of your channel can impact how quickly you succeed. Your success can be hindered if you have a bad name for your channel. But, a good name can increase your viewership.

A good channel name has three elements. Let's review them.

Memorable

Good channel names are easy to remember. Remember that there are thousands upon thousands of YouTubers posting videos. You want your channel to be as easy to remember as you can.

You should keep your channel names short and simple. Avoid using numbers, hyphens and spaces whenever possible. A channel name like 'Flan' is a lot easier to remember than 'xZFlannerDaGamer4143Zx'.

Easy To Spell

Read your channel name out loud. How difficult would it be for someone to spell it if they had never heard it? If they misspell even one letter, they'll likely be confused and will eventually stop watching your channel. The more simple it is for them to spell their channel name, then the better.

Brandable

You want your name to be memorable. It should reflect your channel. It would be absurd to call your channel "FPS" if you do not play first-person shooters.

Before You Begin: How to Stay.

I know you are eager to get this entire business off the ground. You're eager to upload videos to your channel and make some income, even if this is a small amount at the beginning. I know that feeling. I was there.

But, before you begin, it's essential to understand the legal side of things. It would be a great shame if you had a successful channel only to have it taken away because you didn't follow the legal rules.

You are probably aware that copyright applies to game content. Using the content of a game without permission is illegal. YouTube will take down your video and terminate the account of repeat offenders if they receive one of these. That sounds awful, doesn't it?

Most copyright holders won't be tempted to go that far so long as they aren't monetizing their videos. I'll say it again: if you don't place ads on videos, you will probably be in the clear.

Don't worry. You can still monetize them, but not yet. For now, it is best to avoid making money from your videos unless you have the permission of the copyright owner. Be sure to verify that you are allowed to upload nonmonetized games.

You must be 18 years old or have written parental permission to monetize the videos.

You must play safe and obey the rules to avoid losing your entire fortune. Your decision.

Chapter 1: Equipment

Unfortunately, the world we live in is one where everyone expects excellence, even when they're just getting started. To be successful in this competitive sector, your laptop's webcam and microphone are no longer enough. You will have to invest a little money in recording equipment.

Don't be alarmed, though - the equipment will serve you well for many years and pay for themselves before you know it.

Even though this is a short chapter it is still important to understand. Your equipment will make all the difference between success and failure.

Let's get rid of the "did it happen with a potato?" remarks and get some high-quality equipment to record your videos.

Your Gaming Platform

First and foremost you need a platform to host your games. This you know, of course. Today, the most popular platforms for gaming videos today are the PS4, Xbox One Wii U or PS4. But, you are free to use any platform.

This book assumes that you use a PC. That's because PCs are the most commonly used for video gaming (and most games). Some platforms may require you to use specific equipment, rendering this section useless.

If you use a console system, make sure to check what equipment is available and get the best possible price. Let's talk a little more about using a personal computer.

There are good chances that your computer can run smooth games. It's important that you understand that the recording software that is used will require extra RAM.

Recording with the software will require that you close other programs on your computer that are lower-end.

I recommend buying a PC with the best graphics cards and at least 8 gigabytes worth of RAM when you buy a new computer to make gaming videos. This will allow everything you do to run smoothly, with no lags and no hiccups.

Screen Capture Software

There are two kinds of software that I recommend when recording games.

Fraps, the first program is what you'll see. It is likely you have heard of it if any of you have ever watched gaming videos. It's perfect for gaming videos as it's light - it doesn't consume too many system resources. You'll experience less lag, hiccups and other issues while you play which is something we want to avoid.

Camtasia, the second piece is software. Camtasia, although it's expensive at first, will eventually prove to be a valuable investment. Fraps may not be able record every single game. Fraps won't record every game, which can lead to frustration!

Camtasia makes a great backup, as it records the content directly on the screen, rather than what is in the application.

Begin with Fraps. Next, purchase Camtasia when the price feels right. Buy it now if your budget is large. Your call.

How to Choose A Microphone

Next, choose a microphone. This is a crucial step if you want to be heard by your audience. Your words, and not the actual game content, are just as important. You want people to be able connect with you through your videos. Therefore, a microphone is critical to this end.

A condenser mic is better than a dynamic one. This will enable your voice to be recorded without the need to lean over your microphone, or speak at a high volume.

Because these microphones pick-up a lot of background noise, they need to be in a relatively quiet place. This means that you should use headphones to record your videos. The microphone will only pick up your voice, and not the game. (This is what your capture software will record).

There are many microphone options available. You can spend as much, or as little as your budget will allow. A Blue Snowball condenser microphone is on the low end and is often used by commentators. Blue Yeti can be purchased by people who have more money. This mic is slightly better in terms sound quality.

If the case is either one of these, make sure you get the included pop filter. A pop filter helps to eliminate popping noises that microphones may make when picking-up certain sounds. These filters can be purchased for a small amount of money and are well-worth it.

Selecting a Camera

Although it's not essential, YouTubers often choose to showcase themselves in their videos. This allows viewers connect with them more and lets them show how they react during certain events.

There are many misconceptions regarding purchasing a game camera. Many people feel they need to spend a lot of money to get a good webcam.

Most videos with a video camera recording only record part of the footage. Often, the uploader can only be seen in one corner. It is important that the game and not the uploader are the main focus of the video.

This means you can afford a lower quality camera. A camera that records at 1080p or 720p won't make a difference to the quality of your view. It's possible to find a webcam which can record at 480p. Quality will still look great, and it won't cause any additional strain to your system.

Logitech C920 is an excellent choice, both for its low price and great quality. Recording at 4880p is very efficient, and everything runs smoothly.

However, you don't necessarily need a camera if that's what you want. While some people enjoy using them, others may not. Do what works for yourself, and don't be afraid to change.

How to purchase and use a green screen

For those who are truly passionate about going above and beyond what is possible, you might consider purchasing a greenscreen kit. If you're unfamiliar with the capabilities and benefits of a Green Screen, I can tell you that they're quite amazing.

With green screens, you can alter the background of your video without having to cut out. This is accomplished by using a Chromakey. It replaces everything that is of the same color (green), with a completely different image.

There are so many possibilities for a green screen and it is great fun. They are great for creating professional videos, especially if you have a cluttered background.

Although a greenscreen is an unnecessary luxury, it can still be useful. It's an option, but it is worth considering.

Software Editor

Last, but not less important is editing software. You'll need to edit the videos. You will need to edit a lot. In fact, editing is more common than recording.

Here's reality. We are all human. We make mistakes. We make mistakes. Your viewers will still expect perfection, despite all of that. They will move on to the next guy if you don't give it to them.

Unfortunately, editing skills can't really be taught by a book. You'll learn them through your own experience. Soon you'll become a professional editor of video.

It starts with your editor software.

Depending on the budget, there are three kinds of software I recommend. Even though the software may be more costly than the other equipment, it isn't something you should cut corners on. It would be very disappointing if you needed to upgrade your software as soon you become familiar with it.

But, here are my suggestions.

Low Budget: Windows Movie Maker (0)

Windows Movie Maker, which is free and available for Windows XP or earlier, can be used by anyone with Windows XP. This little piece of software doesn't offer much beyond the ability to cut clips and add intros or endings. You can convert your video into HD format. It's still useful.

Windows Movie Maker is a very basic software and you should buy more expensive software. If your channel does well, you will have to do it sooner rather than later so make sure you start it now.

Mid Budget: Sony Movie Studio 13 Platinum ($50)

For $50 you can get some very good software that will enable you to do virtually anything with your video. Sony Movie Studio is an excellent program. I haven't had to upgrade in years. Sony Movie Studio is a solid option for beginners and intermediate editors. Also, it is much less expensive than Sony Vegas.

This software offers the best balance between features, price, and is the one I recommend most to new users.

Sony Vegas ($300), Large Budget

Vegas is the best option for those who are rich and have an incentive to use Sony Vegas over Sony Movie Studio. Sony Vegas is not something that I have had much experience with. The software is loved by professionals, however. It is something I think you will love if you have the means to afford it. But, you might be spending your money better elsewhere.

Chapter 2: Building An Audience

You have a plan. You've learned how to use the equipment necessary for creating amazing videos. Perhaps you've made a few and are now ready for others to enjoy them.

It isn't easy. If your videos don't get viewed often, they won't be able to make a difference. This chapter will give you tips and tricks to make your videos more popular and to build a loyal subscriber base that will continue to view them.

This is the critical section that most people ignore. Although this is not the most pleasurable work, it is what will allow you to be different from thousands of other gamers.

The viewers will be there once your channel starts to grow without you asking. This chapter will help to make your channel more popular so you can spend more time making great videos.

Let's move on!

Understanding YouTube Search Results Ranking System

YouTube's search engine results will bring you most of your new viewers. YouTube's search tool allows you to type exactly what you are looking for in the box. YouTube then pulls up a list that is similar to what you have typed. YouTube doesn't know how to determine which videos are shown, or in what order.

This is because there are so many variables that can affect it. Let's see some.

Keywords

We begin with the most fundamental ranking factor: keywords. These are the keywords that appear within your title, description or comments.

YouTube's search engines have no way of knowing the contents of your video. Therefore, it will make its best guess based on the information that you provide.

It's essential to clearly describe your video. Don't be lazy with the description. Keep in mind that the more descriptive you give about your video, then the more keywords it will appear on the search results pages.

Viewer Engagement

Google intends to give YouTube users the highest quality, most relevant videos. They want people see videos they love. That makes sense. People who like what they see make more money, as they spend more time on the site.

YouTube can't know the quality and quantity of the videos that you upload, but the viewer engagement gives them an indication.

This can be measured via a variety metrics, such as:

Likes and Favorites What percentage of people like your videos? What's your ratio of likes to hates? The higher the ratio, it's better.

Comments. Are your viewers interested enough in your video to give you a comment?

Retention. How long do your videos last? Are they likely to stay with them until the end of your videos or are they often swiping away quickly?

Subscriptions. How often do people subscribe to your videos after they've watched them?

Social Shares: Are others sharing your video via social media? If they are, it is a great indicator to YouTube of YouTube's quality.

Channel Authority

Channel authority is a very important ranking factor. This means the channel authority, which is a huge ranking factor, will automatically rank higher than the one you are on.

It makes sense: who is more likely be creating amazing videos? The guy with 100,000 subscribers or someone who is the first to release their video? Take a look at it.

This is a classic example where the rich get richer while the poor get worse. However, this will work in your favor as you grow into an authority.

A few factors can determine the channel authority.

YouTube believes you are more influential if there are more subscribers.

Backlinks – These links are to your videos and often appear as embedded videos on other websites. Google might see a hyperlink to your video on a website. This will act as a hypothetical "vote," telling Google that the video is high-quality.

Total views: The more views your videos get, the higher they rank in YouTube search.

Your other video history - If other videos have a strong track record of quality and high engagement, YouTube will be more likely to consider you an authority. It's essential to ensure each of your videos are top-notch. It is important to make your channel great and not just individual videos.

Utilizing Social Media

Chances are you use social networks daily. This is Facebook, Twitter, Google+.

However, you might not know that you can use them for business purposes as well as as an incredible tool to help grow your following and drive people to your videos.

If you do not have a Facebook or Twitter account, I highly recommend you make one. Each of these networks will be very useful and beneficial. The sooner you start, the better.

This does two things.

It offers your viewers a way to connect with your videos and to build relationships.

Second, social marketing can make viral videos. If you share your video on Facebook and your fans like it, they will likely share it to their friends. If it's liked by their friends, they might also share it with others. You suddenly have thousands of people watching your video, and they are subscribing. Your video has become viral.

This happens more often that you might think. It doesn't even require many page likes, followers, or fans to make it possible.

Social media can be used to make connections with people on a deeper level. This does not mean posting just links to your latest videos. This means that you should ask questions, get opinions, and engage in a discussion that both you, and your followers, are involved.

Talk about games. Invite your followers. Get involved in the lives of your audience.

One way to improve your social media pages is by using images where possible. Images are great for drawing attention to your posts and allowing people to discover them. A Facebook image is automatically shared to the news feeds of all friends who like it. This isn't true for regular texts posts. Images posts will make your messages more visible to even more people.

Make sure you mention your pages in the description of your videos. That way, people will know where to find them. It is a good idea to link to them within the description of every video.

The majority of your income comes from repeat viewers. Therefore, social media pages are a great way keep people looking at your videos over the years!

Networking

Networking refers the act of partnering other content creators with a view to creating mutual benefits for both.

In other words, you help people out, and they assist you back.

This is hugely beneficial because you can reach completely new audiences. This is a way for you to instantly reach new people.

This is, as one can imagine, very beneficial.

How do you get there? It's really not difficult.

First, you must find people that are open to networking with you. This should be someone with a similar niche and a greater audience than yours.

You can leave them helpful and friendly comments in their videos. Be nice to their videos. Subscribe. Be helpful and do what you can.

28

After a while it's possible to escalate the conversation to text messaging. Make friends with them. You might eventually be friends with them.

If they have a loyal and satisfied audience, their audience is more likely to trust their opinion.

This is often called "growth Hacking" in business, as it allows one to get in front and many people at once. Although networking isn't always easy it will pay off in the end.

It is definitely worth a shot!

Utilizing Twitch.TV

Twitch.TV. Unless you have been living under a rock, you are most likely familiar with it. If you haven't, it's okay because you're about learning all about Twitch.TV.

Twitch is basically a streaming website geared towards gamers. Streamers can live stream their gameplay, as well as interact with their audience through live chat. It's an amazing way to interact and engage with other gamers.

It is also an excellent way of growing your YouTube audience.

You have the ability to add your custom messages and links for other networks to each stream. My favorite thing to do is to add a big YouTube logo and link to your channel's page.

Add to that a monthly message that says, "If you enjoy my stream, please subscribing.

You would be amazed at how quickly YouTube subscribers can be gained by doing something as easy as streaming. It's no joke, some streamers have managed more than 2,000 new subscribers in one hour of streaming. It's unbelievable.

Twitch subscribers are a result of people being watching your stream. How can you increase your viewers?

I have discovered that word of mouth is a great way to attract new customers, in addition to using social media networking as previously mentioned.

This is both good and terrible news. It will initially be difficult for viewers to find your stream. Later on, you will have new viewers flooding your stream.

Engagement is the key to maintaining an audience. Keep your viewers engaged by talking to them during your stream. If they didn't want interaction with you, they would prefer Twitch to YouTube.

It is important to stream on a regular basis. If you stream intermittently, your viewers won't have the ability to attend many of you streams (if any) Your followers will tune in when you have a set schedule.

This is very important because Twitch lists the channels with more viewers first. So every viewer that you have will push you even further up the list.

This is how you can make a huge impact on Twitch and YouTube viewers.

Utilizing YouTube Analytics

You already know that your videos are essential if you wish to succeed.

Google has created an online tool that can help you. It's called Analytics.

This tool allows you access to detailed information regarding your videos and your viewers. It includes their age, gender, place, etc.

You might now wonder, "How can this help me?"

You can tailor your videos to most of your viewers. Most people trying to impact their viewers would make their videos for females quite different from what they would do for males.

A similar scenario applies to content. Most people would adjust their content if their average viewer were aged 18 instead of 55.

The way you do this will be up to your discretion and will greatly depend on the content you provide.

Analytics is something you must pay attention too. You might be surprised by what you discover about your audience.

Your 100th Subscriber

Your 100 first subscribers will be the hardest.

In fact, it may take you longer to get your initial 100 subscribers than it does to get your second 1000.

You're not important to anyone when you're a new person. This is a harsh reality, but it's also true.

You're new on the block. You're the new person on the block. Nobody knows what your stuff is worth. You don't need a lot of followers. People aren't talking to your videos. You do not have authority over your channel.

This means you'll need to put in the work to get noticed. You have to do the hard work of manual advertising in order to get those first subscribers.

It's hard. It is. Most people give in just before the ball gets rolling. YouTube's biggest stars never achieve the success they had hoped for.

However, you're unlikely to be one of these people.

No? Good.

You are already a niche player in your market, and therefore have a big advantage in search ranking.

I recommend slowly releasing high quality videos. You want to capture every viewer, but you won't get many of them early.

Your videos need to be above and beyond the rest. The goal is to impress them and make them feel that they have an obligation to subscribe.

Twitch stream multiple times a day. This is a great method to gain subscribers early.

Stick to your schedule, do your best work and the subscribers will follow. They will start slowly, but eventually they will arrive.

And it's over before you know, it's all over.

Scaling It up - 1000 Subscribers, 10,000 Subscribers, 100,000+!

Although 100 subscribers is great, it's not enough. You want more. 10,000 or even 100,000 subscribers. It's great that you want more subscribers, but 100 subscribers is not enough. Darn.

Subscribers grow exponentially. It starts slowly, but becomes more frequent with time. That's great! But how do I get the ball rolling with this?

It all comes down to utilizing your existing customer base.

Every video should have a clear call for action: like the video and share it on social media. Encourage the viewer to subscribe if they haven't.

Remember what you've learned about channel authority. These are all factors which play into it. YouTube ranks videos that are liked more highly. Higher rankings mean more views, which in turn translate to more likes.

"The rich get more" type of deal.

Keep up with social media. There are many ways to grow your following. Direct them toward your videos.

Network. Partner with other larger channels. Increase your reach quickly. The larger your audience is, the more networks you can build with.

Again, the richest get richer. The more viewers, the more power you have in attracting new people.

The key to getting your channel noticed by as many people and as little effort as possible is the goal. You are only allowed to do what works.

I could go on for 100 pages about obscure marketing tactics, but I kept it to the essentials. I prefer that you spend your time actually promoting your videos, not reading about it.

Get out there, and get it done! Stick with it and be consistent, and you'll reap rewards beyond your wildest imaginations.

Chapter 3: Monetizing Your Channel

This is the end. All that you have read up to now has led you here. The moment you see the reward of all your hard work. When you finally begin making money.

There are many methods to make money via your YouTube channel. We'll be covering all of them in this chapter.

Advertising, affiliate sales and even selling tee shirts is all possible.

To be successful, income is not the only indicator of success.

Over my 7+ year experience in internet marketing, many people have quit after only a few months of their channel not making any money. They would have stopped working at their boring 9-5 jobs if they just worked a bit more on their blog. They'd be playing videogames and collecting checks at home. Seriously.

It won't all be easy. Let's get started on the most exciting part this book, how to monetize your channel.

Google Adsense

Google Adsense will be our first step. Google Adsense is Google's advertising program. It pays content creators such as you money for views and clicks that are served on your behalf.

There's no way to know what Adblock is without using it. These ads may appear before or during the video or on the page it is displayed on.

This is the way most people make most of their YouTube income. But it can be more difficult for gamers.

Google Adsense terms state that all aspects of your video must be owned by you. This means you can't monetize a channel without permission from the copyright owners.

People do this even though they don't know better, and these people are eventually banned from Adsense.

I advise you to not immediately monetize any of your videos. It's unfortunate news. After all, you've worked very hard to get your videos online. It would be a terrible thing if your income potential was destroyed early on because you were just too impatient.

You will legally be able to monetize the videos later on via partner networks. Let's take look at them.

Introduction to Partner Networks

Partner networks can be advertising networks you partner with to display advertisements in your video. You can legally earn money by creating videos with these networks because they have permission from copyright owners for most games to display advertising.

Many of these networks work closely together with their partners. This means that they will usually have some type of minimum before you can accept them. For example, 500 subscribers or 5,000 monthly hits.

When your channel begins to flourish, you'll likely be contacted by potential partners to become part of their networks. In some cases, it may be necessary to apply for them. Although all are the same in principle there are some things you should consider before agreeing or declining to be a part of a partnership contract.

Pay: Since you joined a network in order to get paid, it makes sense to look at what they are offering. Partner networks generally pay a fixed fee per 1000 monetized visits (CPM), typically between $3-8. The higher the number, the better.

Contract Length is how long the contract lasts. Although you may have a contract with only one partner network, it is generally binding until the end of your contract. We will talk more about this shortly.

Pay Structure: What the network does with payments. Some networks will pay monthly, biweekly, or on an annual basis (every $100 is one example). Some networks will also delay payments for a month (each month, you get paid the revenue made two months earlier).

Promotion: This network can help you promote and market your videos. How influential are they? Do they have the potential to bring new subscribers and viewers into your channel? How can they improve your content creation skills?

Support: How efficient is this network's support team? How easy can you get help if there is a problem

Additional Clauses. Any other requirements that the network has. Some contracts forbid you from streaming on YouTube. These clauses may be very restrictive, so it is important to pay attention.

Here are some partner organizations worth checking out:

http://Machinima.com

http://Fullscreen.net

http://Viso.TV

http://UnionForGamers.com

http://VyperNetwork.com

How to choose the best network for your needs

This section will determine whether you succeed or fail.

There are numerous horror stories about content creators rushing to sign contracts only for their networks to screw them over.

Please do not rush to sign any contracts. PLEASE.

As your network grows, you will be offered jobs by many other networks. There's no worse feeling than locking yourself in to a contract for one week only to find out that another offer is available.

A long-term, multi-year contract should not be accepted.

Here's one classic example. If your channel is on the rise, you might be considering a contract. Machinima provides a 3-year contract for $2 per month. 6 months later you have tripled your monthly views, subscribers, and begin receiving offers from other networks offering a $6 CPM.

You're locked in at $2 CPM till the three-year mark. There are no exceptions.

This is also very important. This is especially important if you're about to accept a contract from a network. If you are unable to afford a lawyer, wait before you agree.

Contracts are complex and may contain many more clauses than you initially thought. People may be offered lifelong contracts but not knowing that it prohibits them from participating in certain activities with their channel. When they challenge the contract, they face legal action.

The network will win every single time. Remember that a contract must be legal.

It is a business. Don't rush to sign a contract. Instead, have it reviewed and checked by an attorney. I promise you it will save you many headaches later.

Sponsored Endorsements

If you develop influence over a large group of people you'll be contacted by many companies looking for sponsorship endorsements.

This basically means that in exchange for something or a fixed amount ($100, to mention X company), you will recommend or place / utilize something in your video.

This could be anything from specific gaming gear to the brand soda you use when you record. Seriously.

I've seen people get so much free stuff each year that they had multiple PO boxes.

Another man got a full 3000-dollar gaming PC.

I don't know how you feel, but I think it's pretty sweet to get $50 per video to try Mountain Dew and to voice your opinion about a product.

The company may offer you the opportunity to make money from referrals, even if it doesn't pay a flat amount. This is affiliate marketing.

Affiliate Marketing

Affiliate marketing means that you market products from a company and are paid a commission every sale. This usually amounts to between 4%- 50% of product's retail price.

This is known as an affiliate URL, which allows you to track when you make a sale.

A cookie is stored in the browser when an affiliate links clicks. It tells the company that the person referred them. Most cookies are good for one to two months. So if they purchase anything before then, they can earn a commission. Awesome!

So how do these products get promoted? It's quite simple.

First, you must join the affiliate programme for the company selling the products you want. Sign up for Amazon Affiliate Program to get almost any product you want.

After you sign up you will have the ability to create and place your own affiliate links in your description.

It's generally a good idea if you promote something that's relevant to your viewers interests. Perhaps you have an affiliate button that reads "Buy this video here!" or a link to the actual game.

Amazon's affiliate system is great because you can get paid for everything the person purchases within 24 hour of clicking your link. This means that if they click your affiliate link to a gaming site and purchase a new watch for $4000, you earn a big commission.

It's pretty cool! Affiliate marketing can make you more than ad sales in certain instances. It is worth your consideration.

YouTube's policy on affiliate linking is in a gray area. YouTube refuses to clarify whether or not affiliate marketing is against their terms. To avoid any confusion, people should link to their site in the description. Next, they can link directly to the affiliate products from that website.

How to ACTUALLY Receive Donations

Donations can bring in a steady income. If you can, get them.

It is a problem that many people ask to donate, but then do it incorrectly. Here's how it works.

People don't donate for themselves, they donate for you. People donate to get something. Sometimes it's just the "feel-good" feeling after doing something good.

There are many YouTubers. You want your viewers and subscribers to donate to them. You know, there is only so much money!

A reason is a way to persuade someone to give to you. It must have a reason.

This is a good thing for you, as most people don't do it. You don't need to do much at all to win people over to your cause.

Remember what i said to you in the beginning of this book: you, as a person, are more important then the actual game that you're playing. Your gaming videos should be watched for YOU. The games are secondary.

Engage with your viewers on an individual level if you want donations. You should give donors an opportunity to get more intimate with you.

There are many options. Perhaps you could invite them all to a exclusive multiplayer gaming forum for donators. Perhaps you could have a one-hour per week hangout where all of your donators can speak with you and answer any questions.

It doesn't matter. It doesn't matter.

Keep it in writing and upload it to let non-donators see!

Keep at it and money will continue to pour in. It is that simple.

Selling Merch

If you have a passionate following, you may consider selling merch. This can be done by using your own artwork, slogans, or logos to decorate objects such as shirts, coffee mugs, etc. They can even be sold online.

This is great for passive revenue as well as advertising your channel. It's very funny to think that every person wearing a shirt with your channel logo on it is basically an advertisement for your channel!

Selling merch can be as simple as selling coffee mugs, despite how scary it might sound. There are many platforms available that let you design and host products while also handling customer service and sales. This allows you to upload your product design, and the rest is taken care of.

It doesn't take a lot of people to make this work. It doesn't take a lot of viewers to be a success with this - you just need people who enjoy your brand and would wear it proudly.

This is possible if you're friendly.

TeeSpring, Zazzle or both are great options for selling tee-shirts. CafePress allows you the possibility to sell other products such as posters, coffee mugs and more. It's free!

Links:

http://TeeSpring.com

http://Zazzle.com

http://CafePress.com

Building a Blog

If you are serious about making money online, you might think about creating a blog.

A blog is simply a place where you publish written articles on various subjects (game reviews, personal updates and your own opinions about current issues, etc.).

It not only serves as a tool to communicate with your visitors, but also allows you to send new viewers to the channel when people search for your articles in search engines.

You can actually make a lot of money blogging. This is due to the many opportunities for monetization.

If you are interested to start a blog, James McAllister is a great choice. I recommend his book, "Blogging Profit: A Beginner's Handbook To Starting Your Very Own Web Business", and his website, HelpStartMySite.com.

His book, "How to Build a Blog That Makes Money", is the best. He's an industry leader. He is the best person to show you how a blog can make money.

It is worth considering. Because the upsides of a website are vast and setting one up is much simpler than most people realize. It is not difficult to start a website today, unlike 10 years ago. In fact, it only takes a few minutes to get one up and running.

It's a great way to expand your reach and keep growing your business. Seriously.

This is certainly something to consider!

Chapter 4: Question

Making money online is easier than ever. Today, people can make a lot of money doing what they love and still provide value to others through entertainment or helpful information. It is possible to make six-to seven figures a years sharing information on blogs, playing videogames before an audience or making YouTube videos. Social media can also be used as a lead generation source. Today, there are no limits to what you can do.

Before you begin reading, you must commit to implementing the ideas from this book. It is important to remember that this book will not help you if you don't put them into practice. However, if these are the paths you have chosen, I can assure you that they will help guide you.

There's never been a better time to follow your passion and make money. As you will learn later, these earnings are not just the sum of one income source. They are also the cumulative result from all sources. It is possible to do what others have done. You shouldn't be afraid to try. The key is to be consistent, persistent, patient and do the right actions. Before we dive into the details of making a living playing videogames for a living, it is important to ask two important questions.

Question 1

Before I answer this question, I want me to explain one important concept. Please, please, remember this concept at all times. Your brand will grow as you go along this journey. Everything you do, or don't, will have an impact upon your brand and ultimately your ability to monetize. You have almost no limits on how much you can make from playing videogames.

In fact, you could potentially make up to 2 or 3 million a year. It is becoming increasingly popular to do this. If your knowledge of the most popular games (e.g. League of Legends or Hearthstone) and your familiarity with the most prominent personalities, you will be able to see exactly what I am referring too. Most of them make seven figures per year.

These personalities share the same traits: They are able build a brand around who they are, build a loyal audience around their personality and build authority within their niche. Then, they can monetize on any opportunities that arise. To make a great living, it doesn't necessarily mean you have to be the best in your chosen game. Becoming the best at something may prove to be a poor decision.

The goal of being the best player at your chosen game might bring you a few tournament prizes and sponsorships that may pay the bills for a few more years. But what is your plan once you've achieved your peak in competitive games? It's short-term, but it doesn't have long-term perspective. It is, in other words, a short-term solution that solves a long term problem.

Today, many pro gamers retire before reaching their peak. This is because they know there are better ways than the traditional way to make money in this field. They set up YouTube channels, become Twitch streamers and start their own podcasts. They concentrate on building their audience and their brand and can therefore make 10x as much as they attract more sponsorships.

This is vital, it is what will determine how much you can earn playing videogames. Your ability attract a loyal audience and to monetize your brand effectively. This is the only sustainable long-term gaming strategy. You must remember this, as it is what ultimately you desire to be able do.

How much money are you able to expect to make?

It is the ability to reach as many people as possible with your content that first determines this. It is important to play a popular, well-known game in order to position yourself for success. It doesn't even have to the most popular. However, there must be at least a few hundred thousand people playing it. League of Legends or Dota 2 are some examples of such games. These games are being played by millions every month, week, or daily. If something radical changes, or if game designers make poor choices and lose their audience, things will not change much for at least ten more years.

It is possible to choose either a well-known game or one that's still in its infancy but has great potential. The second option is better because it doesn't involve dealing with other content creators or streamers that have already established themselves as top-tier streamers in the popular games.

The more players that play the game, and the greater your chance of making more, the better. It really is a numbers sport. I would recommend that you steer clear of games that are too niche-oriented, especially flavor-of'the-month, as they can quickly die out after only a few weeks. These games can be very tempting. However, they will not lead to a steady income. Your efforts should be directed in the right direction.

The second factor that can determine how much money your brand makes is the way you monetize it. This book contains a chapter that is dedicated to making sure you have the most revenue streams possible. Every popular player has done it. There's no reason you shouldn't. However, you won't need to build a huge following to become successful or even make a regular income. Let's examine some math. This will allow me to illustrate your potential earnings even if you have a few thousand people.

Let's imagine that you have a small or medium following, and that you are using 6 styles of clothing to generate revenue. You are streaming on Twitch.tv. Also, you have YouTube. You sell your apparel to your followers, you have affiliate programs and branded videos. Additionally, you offer coaching/consulting per an hour in the game of choice. Let's examine each one in detail so that we can estimate how much you can earn from a medium-sized following.

Streaming on Twitch.tv

Twitch.tv remains the most profitable streaming platform. It's a must-have platform, where you can establish yourself on a daily base. Donations are the most effective way to make money. This is the best way to make money as a streamer. People who enjoy you and your style and are open to donating small or large amounts of cash as a way of supporting you, or just to interact with your followers.

Most streamers make well in excess of $6000 a month from this source. Some streamers have reported making more than $50000 from one donation. However, it is not a reliable source of data. You can expect to collect $300 to $1000 per month from donations with a medium-sized audience of between 500 and 1000 streamers.

It works because people are more likely to give you their positive energy and bring value to their lives. Twitch.tv also offers a way to make some extra money by becoming a Twitch Partner. Twitch partners are granted the privilege of a Subscribe button. This allows users to subscribe to your stream for $5 per monthly. You initially split this revenue 50/50, but as you grow your audience you get a bigger cut. Based on your Twitch.tv contract, if your streaming is successful and you manage to attract 100 subscribers, you will receive an additional $250-$300 per monthly.

Once you are approved for their partnership program, you will be able to place ads on your stream. Initial rates are fairly low at $0.80-1 per 1000 views. But as you grow, you will see your ad rates rise to 2.00 or even 3.

For a moment, let's imagine that your ad-rate is $1 per 1000 views. Let's also assume that your following is small. You could expect to make $300 extra per month if your stream is only 5 days a semaine for 10 hours. That's a lot of money for just clicking one button a day.

Owning a YouTube Channel

Let's say that you have a YouTube channel and you upload full video commentaries, stream highlights and any other useful content to your target audience. If you decide to monetize your videos (which you should), you can expect to make around $3 per 1000 monetizable views. If you are partnered by the right gaming networks, you can expect to make $3 per 1000 monetizable view (1000 views on the ads for your videos).

Curse for gamers is one such example. Their partners get approximately 10% of your earnings. You make $2.70 for each 1000 monetized views if they are partnered with you. You think that is amazing? If you can get around 200 000 views per week (which is very easy if the content is great and you follow the content promotion strategies in Chapter 6), then that's an additional $540 per year of passive income. Again, this assumes that you have an average to small following. You will make more money the more views that you get.

One-hour Coaching/Consulting

Offer some type of online coaching, such a review of someone's gaming or a consultation. This is a tutoring gig and you can expect to charge anywhere between $30-40 an hour. These fees are $500 extra per month if 15 are possible (which is the case once you have established an average following).

Selling your Own Apparel to Your Audience

Once you have started selling your apparel (t-shirts/hats, sweatshirts/pants, etc.), you can start making money by selling them to your audience. Your audience will love it, trust me. They will appreciate you making them available so they can help you.

Although you can make an arrangement with a clothing manufacturer and negotiate a deal, it is possible to use spreadshirt.com to distribute your products. Spreadshirt.com will take care of all your shipping, logistics and customer support. They also make sure that you are making a profit on every sale of apparel you make through them. Depending on what material you use and what pricing you choose, your average price per piece can be anywhere from $8 to $15. Even if only 50 pieces are sold each month, that's an additional $600 you can make with a medium-sized customer base. It's a good deal, right?!

Affiliate Programs

Let's imagine that you use these on your blog and in your Twitch stream. This is another passive source of income. If a fan uses the links you provide, you will receive a % of that sale as commission.

Depending on your search efforts, you may be able to find more codes and commissions. I recommend the Amazon Affiliate program at a minimum. However, you could expand to other areas. Most items will pay between 4% and 10%. You can get paid for everything they purchase through Amazon once they click on your Amazon link.

They will make a $500 purchase and you will earn a small commission. With a small to moderate following you should be able to expect to make between $400 and $500 per month. Medium followings, however, can sometimes earn over $1000 per year. Amazon's shopping experience is somewhat luck-based. It is impossible to predict how much someone will spend. There are some people who buy many things at once.

Making Branded videos

These are some of the best ways to make money through YouTube videos. This is the best way, and you can make $600-$700 depending how much you promote in your video. It is quite simple. You simply connect with someone in your niche and see if they offer a product you might like to promote.

Any brand that has a decent following will welcome you to collaborate with them. They may ask for your opinion on a piece they sell of gaming equipment, a piece software or clothing. They might offer you money or even send the product free of cost. This is an excellent way to get new microphones or keyboards for free and make money while promoting them with your followers.

This can be done weekly or biweekly. You will normally charge $100-$200 for each sponsored video. The price of a video can go up depending on your brand's growth. Famebit and other companies can connect you with such brands that are willing to pay money for your advertisement. This can quickly grow into a significant source of revenue.

As you can see from the above, you don't necessarily need a large fan base to make a full-time living while playing videogames. These are just six possible ways to monetize and brand. Next chapter will reveal many more ways you can make even greater money. The examples in this chapter are just to make it clear what you can expect. And I know that you will.

Question 2 How long will you need to make a fulltime income?

Now that I've shown you how much you can expect to make with an average following, the next inevitable question to ask is how long it will take to get there.

However, if your attention has been focused so far, the real issue is: How long do I need to build a loyal follower? Remember that the more loyal customers you have, you make more. This is the goal.

It takes approximately 6 months for a loyal follow to grow if you do the right and work hard. If you're willing to put in the effort and work hard, it can be done in four to five months. It won't happen overnight. Loyal followers are built over time. You must show that you are serious about what your doing and that entertaining people is a priority in you life.

This is a crucial point. It is important to be persistent, and to continue to produce quality content, people will come back for more. Even if a video is awesome and millions of people watch it, if they don't continue to provide great content that their audience wants to see, they will lose patience and move onto your competition. It's the creators who are willing and able to entertain their viewers on regular basis. These people might not be available again.

It is also dependent on your ability and willingness to market your content and promote it to others who may be interested. This includes the use social media platforms. The next chapter will be dedicated to how to promote and market your content to your target audience. If your content has enough quality, it shouldn't be difficult to get people talking about it and sharing it with their friends. There are many options and you can use them all to your advantage.

The average time it takes to have a full-time job is 6 months. Do the right things over several weeks and your business will grow organically through people sharing your content on social media.

We're done with this. Let's look at the ways you can make your money!

Chapter 5: Your Income Sources

I hope by now you realize the importance of building a brand. And that your ability earn money is directly related to your ability create a loyal following. This chapter will discuss 21 different ways to make money with the games that you like. It is possible to build a highly profitable company model using all of them. You can pick which suits you the best but ensure that you have multiple streams of income in order to make maximum profits over the long term.

The goal of the first step is to test as many methods as possible to determine which produces the best results. There may be times when some ways work for you better than others. As your business model changes, you can add or remove things. Make sure you are creative when you use these monetization methods and that you stick to what is most effective. Don't forget to ask your followers for feedback so that you can improve things. Don't let your business model stagnate, keep it flexible in order to maximize your potential for success.

Here are my suggestions for making money.

1: Make YouTube Videos, and Monetize them

This one was already discussed in the previous Chapter. Video content is everywhere today. The number of videos viewed every minute is increasing by the day, with thousands of hours being watched. Every business owner and every brand are trying to use video in one way or another. Chapter 4 will explain how to create videos and record gameplay. However, my book Your Blueprient for Success with YouTube will provide detailed information on how to grow your YouTube channel quickly. To learn more, see Chapter 4.

This is it. First, you must be a YouTube partner. Your account must be at least 30 calendar days old. It should also have been verified and in good standing. Make sure you don't have any copyright concerns against you. You also need to enable it for monetization. It's a quick process, takes just a few minutes.

Next, contact a gamer network (I like Curse – Union for Gamers) in order to monetize the content of your games. For them to accept new partners, you will need to meet the criteria. These are typically quite low. You will receive a portion of the CPM from advertising your videos. I explained this in the previous section. If you missed it, just go back to it and reread it.

2: You can sell merchandise associated with Your Brand

This one is simply amazing. This is a great way to brand yourself in front your target audience.

I strongly recommend that you don't deal with a clothing manufacturer until you have built up a loyal following. It is possible for things to go wrong. You could order too many stock with a poor design and incur losses. You may accidentally damage a piece. Also, large quantities of clothing require too much space. Even if you do it in batches it will still take too much time.

Spreadshirt.com offers a better alternative. Simply create your ideal design, pick your clothing materials, choose your size and colors, and the site will take care everything else. It's so simple and removes a lot from your work.

You will see a decrease in your profit margins for every sale. However, that is okay. You don't run the risk of losing your money, which is better than if it were done all by yourself. It's possible to still make a substantial profit from each sale if you set your price range at around $19.99 to $24.99. If you have a really unique style to sell clothing, you could go up to $24.99.

3: Set up a Blog and Advertisement

This is something very few people do in gaming. It is still amazing to me how many people are missing this opportunity. Blogging can be a great way for people find out about you. Wordpress is free to create.

It's amazing to have people discover your name through the search engine. Post 1-2 articles per Week on topics that are relevant to your audience. These articles can be embedded into your own videos for extra traffic to YouTube. Consider creative ways of attracting people's eye when you name posts. Anything you wish, so long as it's relevant to your target audience's interests, can be discussed.

Cross-promotion on social media is possible. You can promote your own content or videos. There is no limit to your potential, provided you keep consistent. There are many SEO strategies. However, consistency is the most powerful tool. Google will notice if you don't post to your blog for at least one month. This could indicate that Google doesn't believe your blog is valuable for those searching for content related to your niche.

Google stops ranking your blog high in search results, which is the most important way people find your blog. Make sure to keep writing once you launch your blog. The blog posts don't have to contain 5000 words, with gorgeous pictures. Just a couple of articles between 600 and 800 words per week is fine.

4: Add an Membership Section to your Website for Premium Content

Now that your blog is live, you can add premium material to a section of your site and charge users a small monthly subscription to access it. It can be a video tutorial, or an ebook that contains strategies about your game. The value you offer to your audience will determine the type of content.

Premium is something that's unique. Make sure they enjoy it, and that they don't regret spending their money. Please, please, keep in mind that your main goal must be to offer value. If you are able to provide value for their lives, charging them a small amount is acceptable. If the piece is of value, they will be grateful. If it's a sales trick you will make some extra money, but you'll lose a follower.

Keep it updated. Always strive to make your content more valuable and better. If you are unsure how much to charge, it is reasonable to charge $4.99 per month. The price could be as low as $9.99 but you need to make sure it is a valuable piece of content. Otherwise, people might stop subscribing. Again, value is the key.

5: Social Media Marketing with Branded Posts

Chapter 6 of this book gives you more details on what your strategy for social media should look like. As your social media reach several thousand followers, brands may offer to pay you to review the products or services of your followers.

What interaction your posts receive is the most important thing that brands want. Even if they have 10 000 followers on twitter, if their posts don't get enough engagement that's a red signal to them. This could indicate that your followers do not engage in your content, and that you may have sold those followers. These brands will not be fooled. This is why it is so important to have a loyal and engaged audience.

You should be using Pinterest, Instagram, Facebook, Twitter and Twitch.tv as the top social media platforms right now. These platforms are all focused on the visual. Images are what make them viral. Once you have accumulated over 5000 followers, you can start reaching to brands to request that they promote their products.

Trust me, it won't be easy to land every proposal. But even if you do get a few each month, that's still a solid source of income. As you begin to grow, you will discover that the exact opposite is true. Brands will begin to reach out, and YOU will be the one deciding what proposal best fits your audience. Your loyal following shouldn't be exposed to poor products. It's not a good idea. People will quickly react negatively and then leave your channel. Promoting products you are happy with and would use is the golden rule.

6: Sponsorships

Although landing sponsorships and brand deals are not the same, there are some similarities. A brand deal, on the other hand, is a short-term engagement. This means that you promote a product through a post (or video) once and get paid for it. You don't have any further obligations regarding promoting the product.

Sponsorships may be considered long-term arrangements. They are often more difficult to secure, but can yield much greater rewards. They typically include some form of promotional activity from your side, such as a monthly or weekly campaign, in return for a monthly payment plus discounts on products by the company, and other free stuff. Sponsorship deals can be more reliable and lasting than brand deals because they require both your company and your long-term involvement. That's good news for anyone who likes their products.

A second difference is that sponsors won't approach your until you have a bigger following. I mean thousands upon thousands of people following you via social media and YouTube. It is possible if we just keep going. For maximum profits, I recommend combining sponsorships with brand deals. It doesn't need to make you seem too salesy. Don't pitch stuff every chance you get, just be reasonable. Your audience will generally understand why you do what you do, but try not to be annoying!

7: YouTube Videos from Branded Companies

This is similar in concept to advertising on Twitter, Instagram and Facebook. However you will be required to review your YouTube videos.

This can be done at either the beginning, middle, or end your YouTube videos. Brands aren't likely to have any strict requirements about when or how it should be done. They don't care if you place the advertisement. Both services and products can be reviewed.

A second difference is branding on YouTube. You can charge a lot higher than you can for a Tweet. This is because video content tends be more engaging and has a higher likelihood of being shared. It communicates the message better, and also has a visual aspect. While you may charge hundreds for a single minute of advertizing, the price can go up to a couple thousand dollars if your company grows.

8: Crowdfunding

Crowdfunding provides a way for your audience to support and give you small amounts of money. It can be used for funding a specific project or just to support your cause. Today, many content creators see this as their main source or income. Most often, I'm referring to musicians and other artists. But, there are also many video gamers who make it a profitable business.

Patreon is my top recommendation for crowdfunding. Patreon is a place where people can choose to pay a small monthly subscription fee that helps fund you. They can pledge that money to help you fund specific things you publish on Patreon, or they can pledge it for the entire month. However, most people will only support you once a month. It all depends on how much value your contribution. People will happily support you and any of the projects you have if you are creative, funny, entertaining, friendly and a good listener. Join this community.

9: Sell your information products on a blog

Are you really a good player in the game you're playing? It might be possible to sell information products via your blog. That's because digital products are not expensive to make (unlike physical products), can be shipped instantly, and have a high profit margin. It's only important to ensure that your products are of the highest quality. Remember that value is what counts. These items can be priced fairly high, provided they offer value.

Producing information products yourself has the added advantage of letting you decide what to create and how to market it. Another great advantage of producing your own information products is that you have the ability to set your price (and thus profit margin per purchase) depending on the level of value your product delivers to your target audience. If the book is a good one, you can charge as much as $30 per copy. So long as the book is original and valuable. A video course can cost more than $30. However, sales will only be possible if there is a loyal audience willing to purchase your products.

10: Build your email list

Asking any online business owner to name the tool that makes them money the most, 99.99% will respond with email marketing. But wait, isn't email dead? ?

What is the first thing that most people do after waking up? They check their inbox to see if anything is there that they didn't expect or what they need. Email is still a reliable way to reach people in a one-on-1 basis and to advertise to them. This will require a tool. MailChimp is completely free for the first 2000 subscribers. Awebber is an excellent choice, even though many other services are available. They all do an excellent job. It is up to you which one you prefer.

From where can you collect the email address of your audience? Your blog. Give people something in return for their email address. It might be a free report, video, or teaching lesson. It doesn't really matter. Anything that gives them the value they desire will do.

Once you have decided which tool you will use I recommend you send emails to your email address at least twice per week. Be flexible. It may not be enough in all cases. In most cases, it has been what I find optimal. It's okay to send emails once a week. But, you should aim for at least two emails per year. You want your audience's attention to remember that you are still around and that they can contact you.

So how can you make it profitable? You can send videos from YouTube, articles, affiliate links, clothing, and information products to your email list. So that your list isn't cluttered with spam, ensure you always include valuable information.

If you keep trying to sell them things, they will unsubscribe. Remember that the reason they opted in for your email is because they like the content you offer and they want to hear more. Don't misuse that. Give them what they want. But, market your stuff as well. It's a fine line that must be respected.

11: Create a Gaming Tutorial that is Updateable and Get a Monthly Fee

I don't know the game you are playing. It might be League of Legends. Call of Duty. Hearthstone. Dota 2... In any case, the game will always evolve. It could be every few days or every month. But it never stops evolving.

It's possible to make use of that information. You can also create a video tutorial to explain the changes in your blog and give suggestions for how your readers can adapt to the new environment. Or, you can just go through the patch notes. While you have the final say, you can charge a modest fee of $1.99 per monthly to provide quick and easy updates for your customers. Even though it doesn't seem like a lot at first, it adds up when you have 100 people.

12: Have Your Own Weekly podcast

Your podcast is another way that you can monetize and market your brand. You can have it weekly on a specific schedule (let's assume every Thursday at 5:30 EST) but you can also make it monthly. It is up to you. First, this is an excellent way to interact directly with your audience. It's only an additional tool in your arsenal.

Second, podcasts are easy to get sponsors. If you have the podcast recurring each week you may be offered a small payment to promote their products during the podcast. You can invite guests and provide interesting information to your listeners. It's also a great way to have fun and meet new people.

Podcasting has shown amazing results for thousands and it can also be fun for you. It's possible to be surprised by how effective it is.

13: Organize Gaming Events

This is a great way to monetize your website. However, it does require some creativity. Remember that this method of monetizing is only possible if you have a loyal following of at most 50 000- 60 000 people. It won't work unless you do.

You should reach out not just to your own locality, but to all players in the game. Tell them you will organize a contest that anyone can attend for a small donation. If you get enough interest, and you get a great response, you might be able to contact brands that have products that would suit your target audience (keyboard, mouse, etc.) to sponsor this event.

Remember what I've said before: that's exactly how brands want to be seen, through social gatherings as well as exposure to their target markets. You can reach people within the game's communities through YouTube,

Facebook, Reddit or Facebook. Most people are already there. You can offer different prizes in return for the fees that you collect. This usually gets covered by these businesses. A cash prize is also possible, but it's important to get people excited. This will give you the opportunity to meet new people and have fun. It can also be a great way to make a lot of money. I have seen people make well over $20000 from one of these events in the gaming industry.

14: Affiliate Programs

Affiliate programs are a great way to make passive income. Although affiliate programs aren't likely to make a lot, they can be a good way to generate passive income. The commission you earn will depend on what you sell.

I highly recommend Amazon Affiliates. Although there are many, you can use them all. To increase sales and commissions, you can get promotional codes by negotiating.

15: Consulting/Coaching

Are you really proficient in the sport you play? This is a great opportunity to offer advice and guidance to others. Because this is a tutoring position, you can actually make a decent wage per hour. You could easily charge $30 to 40 for a replay review. Or just a consultation to offer solutions to the person's issues.

It isn't really scalable because your hourly wage predetermines. This is where webinars step in.

16: Webinars for Offers

While selling coaching/consulting services on an hourly basis can be a great way make quick money, it doesn't scale well. Create webinars to showcase your expertise. Simply choose a date and set a price. Once they've reserved a place, they can tune into the show and interact with your staff and ask any questions they might have.

Even though you may charge less than consulting for webinars, they offer a group-based experience and coaching. You will also make more per hour. In fact, for a webinar that costs $20, 15 people can tune in and earn $300.

Although you could do the math with more numbers by yourself, I used this example to show how profitable webinars can become.

17: Speaking Opportunities

How can gaming events bring in money? It not only allows you travel, but also provides two types of monetization opportunities.

The first is that speaking at events may be a way to get paid. But, unless you are very well-known, you should not do it. The opportunity to speak at an event related to the game you are playing is a way to get free exposure to people who might be interested in your products. Nothing is better than more publicity. This is because more publicity means more views and followers, higher ad revenues, and greater sales of your products or services. Indirectly, speaking at events will benefit you.

18: Twitch Advertising and Subscription Revenue

I've already discussed this in the last chapter. But, if money is your goal for playing video games then Twitch.tv will be your best friend.

It's the top platform for streaming gaming videos and it won't be changing anytime soon.

Twitch partners are those who reach a certain number. This will give you a few privileges but the most important are the ability to place ads as often and as often you want on your live gameplay. I have explained this already so I won't do it again. In return for $5 per monthly, you also get a Subscribe button. Twitch.tv splits this revenue 50/50 initially (60/40 later as you continue growing), but I assure you that it will increase over time as you attract loyal fans who are more likely to support and share your content.

19: Add an additional donation button to your Twitch channel

As soon as your stream starts broadcasting, you will be able to add a donation button. That's the great thing about Twitch: you don't have to provide any prerequisites. People can interact with each other and send them funny messages, congratulated you on your hard work, and you can also add a donation button to your stream.

Contrary to the subscription deal, you keep all of your donations. Twitch.tv is not required to split them. This feature is worth recommending. It's still one of my favorite ways to make a living streaming live gameplay. The key to success is your ability to attract loyal followers.

This is the essence of the next chapter. It will help you build loyal customers. This is what makes it all work.

20: Get involved in tournaments

Are you good at the game that you are playing? If not, don't worry. It isn't a requirement, but it sure won't hurt.

Participating at local tournaments is a great way to increase your income. It's how you become better than what you have now, by facing others on the same level, or higher.

21: Buy Art that is Related to Your Gaming Niche

Are you skilled at creating art? Are you able create original images, drawings, and designs that are beautiful? These are also possible to monetize. It's amazing to see how many people value art. If you're gifted in this area, don't hesitate to make something for your fans. A lot of them are happy to pay a fair price in exchange to the value they will receive from an original piece of artwork.

These monetization techniques all yield results. Each of them scales as you grow. Literally, the money you can make from them all the faster you grow. YouTube videos monetization will make you more money by attracting more people to your videos. The more popular become, the more you can charge for a consultation/webinar, the more you can demand from the companies that offer you sponsorships.

Same applies to the results from speaking opportunities or gaming events. While you can't make your membership site more expensive, more people will sign up for it. This is a recurring income stream that can be used monthly so you don't have to be overly greedy. If you are a branded video producer, you can expect to receive more money as you become more successful.

This information should be used as motivation to help you build the inner power you need to work hard. As long as you're consistent, hard work and perseverance will pay off.

Chapter 6: How to make your audience loyal and stand out from the rest

I've probably already mentioned how important it is to build your brand. Now we're going to show how to do that: how build a loyal audience, and how stand out from your competition.

I will make an educated guess. It is likely that you assumed that only few people can make it a career out of video gaming. You've probably heard of the professional players, the pros. You may have thought at some point that, unless your skills are exceptional, people won't be as interested in you playing games.

W-R-O-N-G. Your ability and skill to play competitively is not a factor in your success. Remember that content creators are you. It's vital that you give value to everyone who is interested in what you create. You can think of what most people consider a goal when they play a videogame. You would be surprised at how few people think about how much they can do in a videogame. They simply want to relax, have some fun, unwind from a long day at work, and entertain themselves. It is true that the majority of people use video games as a means to relieve stress.

They want entertainment. Most people don't care about your level of skill, as they don't wish to put their efforts into becoming an expert at video gaming. Instead, they're interested in making a difference in their lives and playing video games as a hobby. Now that you have read that, it is clear that video content creators that deliver the most entertainment value are the ones who succeed. This is not a criticism. This does not mean that you should behave in a clownish manner on video or that your content needs to be educational.

When people are able to associate with you, it is because they feel valued. Are they made to feel important by you? They also expect to receive entertainment value for their time. When they watch your video or listen to your stream, it is investing in you. That's the most precious resource one can have. It doesn't matter what your skills are in casting spells and killing minions. What matters most is whether you make them smile, if you engage with them and answer any of their questions. Now let's discuss the details of building a loyal fanbase.

What does it entail to have loyal followers?

First, let me tell you about what makes a loyal following. It is not about the size of your following. It doesn't make a difference how many people have followed you on social media, or how many subscribers to your YouTube channel. Those numbers are just numbers. A statistic. Although they might seem impressive (or not), they aren't what will determine your success.

It matters how invested people are in your brand. How many people sit impatiently waiting for your next video? How many people are just waiting to send you a message on social networking to say "Thank You!" for the positivity and smile you brought into their lives. How many people want you to know that they are happy for you and would like to congratulate yourself on reaching this milestone?

How many people will defend your reputation when you're criticized. How many people will go above and beyond to share your content or buy your products? How many people would kill to have you hug them, shake their hands or hold their hand? I could go on and on, but the point is clear. This is what your goal. These are the type of reactions you want. This is what success looks.

Pick a particular niche you love and stick with it

First, find a niche that you like to work in. Stick with it once you've determined what it should be. Stick to one genre (MOBA, RPG), and only allow for entertainment or educational purposes. Whatever you choose, it will become your brand and define who you really are. This is why you must adhere to it. Because every new video or piece of content that you produce will allow you to reach and attract new viewers who are strictly interested in the content.

You can attract people who are most interested in entertainment by making a fun and entertaining video. People who are interested more in education will prefer informational videos. If you stick with the same content type you will improve your skills and attract the right people.

This is what I see a lot when content creators try to make money playing videogames. They have no target audience. First, they would create an entertainment clip, then a full-game commentary, then some tutorials and finally a vlog. They attract non-targeted subscribers who visit their channels only for that one piece, like a tutorial. They never find a niche audience that is willing to watch everything they produce.

These people are the ones who end up having 50 000 YouTube subscribers, and just 2000 views for each video. It's a horrible position to be in. Because when new users discover a channel like this, the first reaction they have is "Wow 50 000 subscribers and only 2k viewers per video?" The content of this guy must be awful or he bought the subs." No one is going to give you a chance.

Please, please, do not fall for the trap. The good news is that you can diversify your content as your audience grows. Once they reach the hundreds of millions, people will become so used to your brand that they don't care about what game you play and what platform you use. They will follow where you go. This allows you to be flexible, and allow for more variety in your content.

Identify Your Target Audience

Next, choose your niche and identify your ideal target market. What are their genders and ages? What is their relationship status? And how much time can they expect to have per day? What language does each speak? What do they look for in a video stream or a streaming video? What are they passionate about? What kind of personality do these people have? What makes them different? Whatever it may be, define clearly who your target audience looks like. This will set the stage for your strategy in attracting them. So that you can gain the most understanding, be precise in your terminology.

This is critical because you want your viewers to say "Hey, this was amazing!" This is the content I was looking at!" It will greatly improve your results. Doing all of these things will help you to eliminate a lot more of your competitors. There are tens to thousands of people making gaming videos. However, a smaller number of these people will relate to the content your target audience (which has been clearly defined) wants. This is the way to get rid of your competition.

Consistency

With regards to building a loyal follow, consistency is the next important concept. The number of creators that fail to update their audience with new content over time is something I can't count. You'll understand what I mean. A creator uploads a wonderful video. People love it and share it.

However, after a week or so nothing happens. Then they make another video. Next, it takes 2 more weeks for them to upload anything. They then went on an endless uploading spree, for about 2 weeks, to try to "make-up" for their inconsistency. Only to burn out after that and not upload any content for a whole month. Soon their subscribers are fed up and quit. It's not possible to build a following of loyal subscribers unless your actions show that you care about giving them consistent access to the content they love.

If you sit idle for long periods of time without getting back to them, they'll realize that producing content for their needs is not a top priority. And they will just find someone who will. Inconsistency is what I believe is the most important reason people give up on the gaming business. It's not their lack of skill or talent. It's their inability of sticking to a schedule, and satisfying their audience's needs. You must remember that the people you attract are not numbers. They are real people. You may never see them again.

How can you do this? It's easy to pick a schedule that you want people to be aware of. It doesn't necessarily have to be something outrageous. You don't need to stream or make videos every day. You just need to pick one and stick to that. If you have 3 videos per week and three streams per semaine, that is fine. Be consistent with your schedule. Otherwise, your audience may feel betrayed.

I get it. Sometimes you get sick or need to travel, and videos are impossible. We all have to deal with the unexpected. Instead of keeping it private, inform your audience you are away for a date or you are ill so they can not stream/make videos. You can trust them to support you and to understand you if this is something you do.

Another option is creating an extra 2 week worth of content that can be saved on your harddrive to use for these kinds of occasions. You can simply refer to the "reserve" whenever you feel unwell. Your audience will never know. Make this your career and be serious! You must set a time and stick to it. There's no excuse!

Frequency

Your schedule should be scheduled with some frequency. With so many competitors around, it is vital that you remind your viewers about yourself regularly. The minimum number of videos uploaded per week is enough to get decent results. But, going in the opposite direction and uploading content three times per day on YouTube will just frustrate your viewers.

They will soon feel overwhelmed by all the content being sent out, and they will eventually unsubscribe. Aim for a medium number of videos per week. I suggest streaming 5-6 days per semaine for at most 6-7 hours. Once people are more familiar with you, they will start to be interested in more of your content.

Quality (of the content)

This one is obvious but I won't deny it. You should provide your audience with high quality content. This type of content is connected to the concept Frequency. In other words it is better to post less videos and stream more but have higher quality content.

The rule is to choose quality over quantity. A lack of quality is a big deterrent, especially for those just learning who they are. It shows you don't necessarily care about providing value.

Content you produce must be relevant. It should make people smile, laugh, learn or have a positive impact on their lives. You should treat everyone in your audience as a million-dollar client. Your goal is for them to have the best viewing experiences possible. This includes streaming high-definition video (720p and 1080p), as well as having stable internet access (bandwidth), to ensure your stream doesn't lag.

Your microphone and camera should be high quality so that people can clearly hear and see your voice. Is your graphics card fast enough to avoid "lagging" and allow you to play at low frame rate all the time? How is your ability to speak and give commentary? Are you working on them, if not satisfied? Are you asking your followers for feedback to help you improve?

How are your editing skills? How much time have these skills been taught to you? What are some cool effects you can add to your videos? Have you made great graphics for your YouTube channel and Twitch channel art. How do you look in your profile image? Do you look your best on there? What about your social posts? Are you sharing meaningful content that will be of interest to your followers on social media? Do you make sure to update them on the happenings around you, in case they are curious?

My point is: Quality doesn't always have to revolve around video production. Look at how quality can be added in every aspect of your work that relates to the audience. If you can think like that, you'll be so much further ahead than others!

Show your appreciation for everyone you meet.

As I stated, the people who might be interested is your content isn't just numbers. They are human beings with feelings. They want the feeling of being important. That is why they are so interested in social media. They want their voice to be heard and to feel that someone cares about them.

Ask questions! Imagine this: If you've gained a certain amount of following, you can be considered a person of authority for that group. Do you think it would make people feel important and valued if someone in your place asks for their opinions? It most likely will. People will feel honored to be asked about their opinions and will share theirs with you. This is the key to engaging them!

What are you supposed to do to show your appreciation for their efforts? First, thank them often for following you around and looking after your stuff. This is the best method to show your appreciation. You could also organize an event for them to participate in to show them how valuable you are. It doesn't have to involve a lot of people. You can do a Google Hangout, or just a big group chat. Any gesture will do.

Collaborating with other creators is another way to go. It might be possible to make a YouTube video and collaborate with someone who your audience likes. Or maybe you can just stream with that person. Another way to do it is through subscriber games. I guarantee your audience will love you for spending the time to have fun with them.

It's also important to show appreciation for your audience whenever you receive a donation, or a new subscriber. Writing whole social media posts relating to your appreciation of your followers is a good idea. A second thing you can do is answer questions in YouTube comments or stream. These little actions are the key to success and must be done on a daily basis. For motivation, keep in mind that it will all be well worth it. Because that is what it takes build a loyal fanbase as a gaming professional.

Let your audience feel that you are a friend and become more connected

You need to be able connect with your followers in many different ways. You should make them feel like they actually know you. You can share your life experiences with them. People don't want you to get too personal. This is because your audience has likely been in the same position at some time. Tell your audience stories and jokes. Let them know about your hobbies, and how you spend your time. Let them know about your inspirations and goals. Tell them about the people that inspire you. Tell them about your motivations, and what are your core values.

You need to remember that even though you may have tried hard to attract a certain audience, the majority of your audience will be in different age groups. While a portion of your audience may still be in highschool or college, others might be attending University or College while others are working full-time raising a family. You can always share a personal experience with your audience, provided it's not too personal.

If you are still high school, talk to your classmates about what is happening in high school. Discuss University life, and what you got up to last night. Please share your last TV episode or soccer game. People will appreciate you sharing your TV show or playing soccer with them. They will feel you trust them. It will result in them being more open to you and your ideas, which is exactly what they want.

Talk to them like you are speaking to your best friend

This is not exactly the same as it sounds. Being more personal with your audience will create a deeper connection than simply being interested in the content. There will always a person who is more talented and creates better content than you. That's the beauty of life. You will always outperform your competition, regardless of how hard you try. But, I can tell you that your competitors will struggle to connect with their audiences because most don't think about what it takes. You would be amazed to find that most creators don't think about it.

Now, when you talk to your audience, you can imagine being your best friend. This golden rule applies to every interaction. Treat others as you would treat yourself. If they have any questions, answer them and thank them. It's amazing how far this can go in your audience-development campaign. It is common for people to not feel that sense of attachment in the real world. This can be due to many factors. Once they connect online with what they need, they will be able find it in their real lives and feel connected to you.

Ask Your Customers Frequently for Their Feedback and Opinion

Take initiative. Ask your audience members about topics of common interest. Do it often. It doesn't have be restricted to gaming or your channel. Try something different and do some personal stuff. Keep in touch with your friends and be approachable. Each day you should strive to interact with them in a different way.

You have to ask yourself how many content creators who are in positions of authority actually do that. How many people actually go out of their way daily to ask questions and then maintain the communication based on the answers? There's no shortage of them, right? This is how it's possible to distinguish yourself greatly from your competition.

Most people don't care enough about their audience. They view those who follow them only as numbers or as potential sales leads. Asking questions indicates that you CARE. Do it every single day, sometimes even twice per day. Don't be inconsistent with this. It will be easy to establish strong connections with those you follow by making dedicated social media posts about such topics.

Listen to your Audience's feedback and give them what they want

When asking your followers questions, pay attention to what they say. All feedback is important. People will tell you if your video is poor. Although there will likely be some hateful comments, most people will leave constructive criticism. It usually relates only to what they believe your content should look.

If you start to see trends, (i.e. Consider what you can see as trends, such as multiple people giving you the exact same feedback on a subject. If it makes sense to you, then you can apply what you've learned the next time that you stream or make video. If the comment is repeated about a tee shirt design or your channel's art, it's worth taking the time to think about. Let's be flexible. Let people have their say and be open-minded. This will allow you to get the results you desire. But don't expect to please everyone. Your goal is to please all people, or at least make it seem like you're trying to please them all.

Negativity and hate are best ignored

You need to distinguish between constructive criticism from hateful and positive comments. Constructive criticism is supported by strong evidence. It has a note that is positive, respectful and is geared towards improving your performance. Negative and hateful criticisms are characterized by trolling, personal insults and insults towards others.

No matter how nice of a person you may be, it is inevitable that you will meet this person at some time. It happens to all of you and the best way is to block that person. You might want to prevent them ruining your reputation by blocking them. Your online reputation is affected by your positive interactions and how you deal with negativity.

The worst thing that you can do is to get into a pointless argument and reply back. It makes you look bad and puts you at risk of being pushed around by others. You might be trolling yourself if others start to notice the conflict.

Keep in mind that this is the internet. Assuming someone is anonymous and secure behind the computer they can freely express themselves to anyone they want, without worrying about the consequences. Learn to take action to stop this behavior from happening in the future. The easiest way to stop people from bothering you and your viewers is to simply block them. Block them from creating a second email account. This will ensure that they don't spread their negativity elsewhere.

Reproach yourself when you screw up

This one might make it uncomfortable for some, but it is necessary. Let's not be naive. There will be many mistakes. Sometimes you will wrongly judge people by misinterpreting what their words say. You may ignore their feedback, or act out of stubbornness and do the exact opposite to what is expected.

It's perfectly okay. As long as your mistake is recognized and you apologize when necessary, that's all that matters. What is the difference between acknowledging a fault and apologizing? It's because you care about what others think of you. Even though you may not be sincere, it's a start. People will appreciate this quality.

Play with your Subscribers occasionally

What could be more fun than playing with your subscribers? While it may not be possible to play with everyone, even if you tried, it would take too much time. Even if you tried, it would cause some people feel isolated and forgotten.

You can do this by creating subscriber games via Twitch. There are several ways this will benefit you. It will make it easier for more people and increase your Twitch subscribers. Because they are more accessible, they feel more invested in you. It's not hard to see why so many people, particularly the top-ranking ones, do it. Do it, too. Even if this is your first step. You will attract more people to yourself if you spend the time with them.

Be authentic

People don't like being lied too. Asking a question should not be interpreted as a lie.

If that's true, simply ignore it. Nobody can force you into answering a question you do not want to. In any case you must not publicly like your audience. It's often easier to detect than you might think. It makes you look fake and negatively affects your reputation. You're completely wrong, I say.

Be kind both online and offline

How often do you see a YouTuber or streamer act as the most kind, sweet person you've ever seen on camera? Then they get offline and start to spew negativity in chat or on other peoples' channels. It's more frequent than you might realize. People will see it and it will immediately reduce your credibility.

It's like lying to your fans. People will see you as fake. This is easy to avoid and many people make mistakes. It is important to be polite online as well offline. Always remember, even if you're playing with other people online, that anyone can see what you have to say.

It doesn't matter if it is a bad day or if it makes you feel annoyed, just be yourself.

Make Cool Things for Your Subscribers that Other Creators Do Not

Your subscribers will appreciate you doing cool things that other people in the same position as you don't. This shows you appreciate them for watching you play videogames. It also shows them that you value them and are committed to making them feel important.

They can take part in interesting little contests. Your apparel can be customized to their specifications. There are many ways you could do it. Spend the time to get in touch with your audience. Use your imagination.

Chapter 7: How to Grow Your YouTube Channel

YouTube is your best friend if you want to make a good living from playing video games. If you have already defined your target audience (please go back to Chapter 1 and do so before you continue reading), there are 99.99% chances that it is already on YouTube. These people are actively looking for video content that interests their interests.

YouTube currently has over a million users. And statistics show that YouTube has the highest reach of any cable network among 18-34 year-olds. In 2016, 500 hours of video was uploaded per minute, as opposed to 72 in 2012. Content creators have never had more competition. Anyone can upload video on YouTube today. If YouTube success is a priority for you, then I recommend you purchase my book, Your Blueprient for Success on YouTube. You can also get it on kindle. It includes all the details of how to quickly grow on YouTube, extra audience growth strategies, and many more.

The Setup

Once we've established that YouTube is mandatory for you, you should create a YouTube channel. To create a channel, click the Sign in button at Youtube.com. Next, enter your email and password. I know you don't want to hear me bore you. It's likely that you've done this several times.

I encourage you to take the time to consider your desired username before you decide on it. I suggest you choose your brand's title, not your real name. Consider that the name of your YouTube channel is what people will associate you with on the platform.

Let me start with the things you should avoid doing in regards to your channel title:

-Don't include numbers

-Do Not use random capitals

-Don't make it so long people won't be able to remember it (no more that 2 words).

-Ensure it doesn't contain anything offensive, or have racial implications

-Stop using too many symbols

Here are some tips on how to choose a channel name

-Select a name to represent you as an individual and content creator

It must be easily understood

-It needs to be unique

It should be in keeping with your target audience's taste, i.e. If your brand is producing entertainment content, you need to include something that relates to it.

Keep it succinct and short. It's easier for people to remember.

-It should be specific, not generic. Remember, it's YOUR brand.

Once you have decided on what you want it to look like, share it with friends and invite them to give their opinion. You might be surprised at how valuable other opinions can be. Once you have decided on the name of your channel you can start moving to the next stage.

Next, buy some quality gaming equipment. Please don't purchase the cheapest items. It isn't worth it. While you don't need to spend money on the most expensive equipment, it is important to have good quality equipment if you want your product to be worth viewing.

First, make sure you invest in a top-quality microphone. While the good quality microphones can run you $40-$80, it is worth it. You will need the mic to record voiceovers, stream online, make questions and answers series, or add commentary to your gameplay. While there are many low-quality microphones, I am aware that they can be expensive. What person would like to hear their voice sound squeaky and unnatural, no matter what the content? Poor audio can discourage viewers, especially those that just discovered your channel. High quality microphones are not cheap.

OBS is my favorite program for recording. You can record anything with it, including streaming. It should include editing software. Keep in mind that editing does require some effort at first. Be prepared to spend some time learning. I would start out with a simpler editing software, such as iMovie. This will allow me to feel comfortable editing.

Once you feel comfortable, move onto something more advanced like Adobe Premiere Pro and Sony Vegas. While it may take some time for you to get to know them, they will be very easy to use. When you start to get comfortable editing, it will become easier to create really cool effects to enhance the quality of your video.

Also, ensure your computer's specs are in line with the requirements of any game you play. It is not necessary to use a powerful machine if you are making video about League of Legends. While any budget laptop should be sufficient, you can play Call of Duty on a faster processor.

A second option is to get an external drive that can store all the videos you have made. Files can be stored in the cloud but I prefer old-fashioned hard drives. They can store several terabytes. Recording in high resolution, which you should, can cause your videos to take up large amounts of space due the large size of high-definition video files. Once you're done editing, it is recommended that you compress the video. By compressing your video before you upload it, you can save a lot of space and speed up the upload process to YouTube.

It is important to have a stable internet connection. This is especially true for streaming but not YouTube. Even though it may not be very fast, ensure it is stable and reliable to stream. A mouse, keyboard, and headphones are all necessary. Once your account has been active for at least a month, verify it, and then enable it for monetization. Congratulations! You have been made a YouTube partner. It is tempting to upload your first video and then start monetizing the video so that AdSense can make you your first income.

Monetizing Videos and Becoming an YouTube Partner

YouTube requires that you have the appropriate license from your publisher in order to monetize the gaming content. In this case, you will be in violation YouTube's terms-of-service and may lose the ability to monetize other content on your channel. How can you get this license? A YouTube gaming network is the best option. They will help you obtain the commercial use rights required to monetize YouTube videos. You'll also receive a small percentage of your advertising income. They can handle all of the legalities. It's annoying that they share a percentage ad revenue with you, but it's necessary.

Gaming networks have certain requirements. You have to meet their minimum view count and subscriber requirements. A majority of networks require you to have 1000 subscribers, or 1000 views per month for the last 30 day in order to be accepted. Based on your contract, the gaming networks usually take around 10% to 40% from the adsense earnings that you earn per month.

Curse/Union for Gamers allows you to take more of your income and offer an open-ended, flexible contract that allows you freedom to leave whenever you choose. They also take 10% of your monthly ad revenue. With the most popular gaming networks, you can expect to make about $3 per 1000 monetized visits. Sometimes, this is even higher. If your network is growing, you may be able to negotiate higher terms. This is because your popularity will influence your network's success. Once you've been accepted into the gaming network, it is legal to monetize videos.

Select Your Target Audience

After you have selected your niche, find out who your ideal target market is. What are their genders and ages? What's their relationship status? How much free time would you expect them not to use in a day. What language do these people speak? What are they looking to see in a stream or a video? What are they passionate about? What personality traits do they possess? What makes them different? Whatever it may be, clearly define who your target audience are. This will set the stage for your strategy to attract them. For the greatest understanding of your audience, you should use very specific terms. Make sure to write at least one page.

This is critical because when people view your videos, they should think "Hey! That was awesome!" This is the kind of stuff that I was looking! Doing all this will effectively eliminate a lot your competition. Although there are tens or thousands of gaming video producers, very few will be able relate to the content that your target audience (which has been clearly defined) seeks. By appealing only to a small group of people, you can easily eliminate your competition.

Your Channel Art

Your channel art will help you brand your channel. I strongly recommend you take the time necessary to create a professional looking banner. The best part is that you don't have to be a Photoshop pro to create something beautiful. YouTube offers many free tools to create banners.

They provide many useful functions that make the process very simple. Include all social media links, Patreon page or Twitch stream. Make sure you include your video schedule as well, so that no one misses it.

If you think that creating it yourself is too difficult, I strongly recommend you outsource it. You can either hire someone with experience and professionalism in this area, or pay someone $5 to do the job for you on

Fiverr. Be sure to be satisfied with their work and you are proud to use the finished product for your brand.

Your YouTube About Page

Here is where I see many creators making mistakes. The majority of people underestimate this part of their channel. Many people overlook this part of their channel. They then wonder why it is not producing good results. Your About page (along with the Channel trailer that I will briefly discuss) should be a brief description and description of yourself, what you hope to achieve on your channel, how viewers can benefit from your content, and a description for your posting schedule.

Keep it simple and succinct. Next, make sure to list the best ways people can contact your company if they have any questions. These include your Twitch.tv feed, your business email address and your post address (not necessary), your blog, all social media accounts, as well your Patreon page.

This simple formula works best for creators. It allows people to learn more about you and what you do. It tells them what you do, how frequently they can expect you upload videos, and how they can reach you. This formula will help you retain your audience over time.

Your Channel Trailer

Like your about pages, your channel trailer allows people to view a short presentation of what your channel does. The only difference between the two is that it is in a video format.

Your goal for your channel trailer is to catch the attention of new visitors. It should be quick, relevant and attention-grabbing. You should keep it between 30-60 second in length so that people do not click away. You have to convince them in 30-60 seconds why you are worth the time. You can add a channel intro. Or, I prefer your best highlights.

Because this is the first impression most people have of you, make sure it's edited well and high-quality. Unimpressed people will leave and go elsewhere. If you hook them, they'll be excited to see what else you have and will subscribe to your channel. If they find that your other content has great quality, they will be able to watch many more videos from you. This is what the goal should be, right?

Your uploading schedule

Do you remember the time I asked you about your schedule and how you listed it in your about page. Because it sets people up for what to expect of you, they must be aware. You can be sure they will continue to receive your content on a daily basis. Think of it as a TV programme that airs every other Sunday at 20:00pm. People know they'll get a new episode each Sunday. That's because of the show schedule.

People will love your content and be more interested in seeing each video that you make. Your viewers will begin to trust you if you keep delivering the content on a regular basis and adhere to the schedule. Because it opens you up to all the monetization strategies I discussed in Chapter 2, trust is a fundamental requirement for building a loyal following.

You can do it the other way. If you promise people you'll post 3 videos per Week, and then go three weeks without posting a single video, part of your audience may doubt your word. You have not lived up to your promises. If you keep doing this a few more time, people will be less likely to trust your words and eventually, they will stop caring about you.

This is why I recommended that you have videos prepared and stored in advance. In case of an emergency, you will always have content ready to upload. There are no excuses not to make this happen. Be prepared, be serious and hold true to your word.

Publishing Frequency

This brings us to publishing frequency. How frequently should you post videos to YouTube? Well, it depends. It depends on how time-consuming editing a video takes, what type or length of video content is being created, how much time you have, how long the videos are, and how much you have available. You may need to make full-game commentaries. These videos will generally be longer. You can expect to be able to comment for up to an hour depending on which game is being played. These videos require very little editing and are easy to produce. I recommend you limit the number of videos you produce with this type of content to around 4 videos per week. If you do, you run the risk to overwhelm your audience. It is not possible for everyone to devote more than 5 hours per week to your NEW content. They might even want to catch up on the old content they already have if they just discovered you.

You can produce 7-10 videos per semaine if you make shorter videos (approximately 5-10 minutes). This may seem like a lot but it's not.

10 videos of five minutes each are less than an hours worth of video per week. This will allow your audience to easily access all your videos without them having to spend their whole day watching them.

Remember that the more your people click on videos, watch and enjoy them, the better they become at watching you on daily basis. If they do this over a number of weeks, it becomes a way of life. As you gain experience, you'll notice that people often check whether there are any new videos uploaded. It's a fantastic feeling to create content.

Whatever frequency you choose, don't change it. It doesn't matter what, keep it up. Take into consideration how long it takes you to produce a movie and determine your upload frequency. If you are working full-time, which you should, then you will likely have all the free time in the world. You can't expect to be successful if you work part-time.

What length should videos be?

Another important factor is the length and quality of your videos. This has been touched briefly in the previous paragraphs. The content that you produce will dictate the length and quality of your videos. To make complete game commentary, make them around 40 minutes to an hr. You can also make entertainment videos in a shorter time frame, which is usually between 5-10 mins. Ten minutes is not enough.

I strongly recommend sticking to the lower part of this spectrum. People today have short attention spans. They tend not to finish videos they started.

It is important to remember that shorter videos will often be highlights, unless they are clips from a longer video. Highlights require considerable time to edit and synchronize correctly, so it is worth considering the time investment. When you want to produce a very high-quality video, it can sometimes take more than 3-4 hours to collect all the material, cut it, add music or voiceover, edit and compress the file.

Trust me, it's always worthwhile as the video will continue to be available on your channel for years. It will make you money even ten years down the line, so long as it continues to be viewed and YouTube is still alive. Do your best work when producing videos, as each one has the potential to pay off in the near future.

Consistency

This brings us to consistency. This is something I've discussed in every Chapter. But I want you all to know how important it really is to remain consistent. I have seen many interesting examples in my own life of consistency being better than being extremely smart or talented, but also lazy and inconsistent.

My experience has shown me that some of my most gifted friends have failed miserably at everything they attempt. It is simply because they are not able to stick with anything. They lose sight of what is important. They take on unimportant "busywork" that doesn't add value. They start new things and never finish them. Then they move onto the next thing. This is a recipe fro failure. I don't really care about how talented or not, consistency will make you fail in all areas of your life.

Yet, I've also witnessed the opposite. It isn't unusual nowadays to see someone with lower than average intelligence, a lack charisma, no social skills or personality reach remarkable heights of success. What is the secret to their success? Because they keep their focus and persevere in their efforts. They wake up determined to complete their tasks, regardless of whether it is easy or difficult. They have the determination and work ethic to stay focused on their goals, regardless of circumstances. They make it a priority for their lives and they persevere.

Your videos won't be the best quality right away. That's perfectly normal. Don't let that discourage you. Just keep going. You will experience discomfort and learn new things along your journey to success. However, it doesn't matter how awful your videos are at the beginning, if that persists, you will soon get better.

You will notice a dramatic increase in your quality over time. The amazing thing is that this happens naturally, without your even realizing. You have to remember that every person who excels at something has been once unsuccessful at it. You will become more proficient at something if you put in the effort each day. It's a well-known formula. It is a proven formula. Keep that in your mind at every stage of your career.

Video Editing

Like all other skills, video editing requires practice. There is a good chance that you will begin from scratch. You'll feel overwhelmed the first time you try it. You will feel overwhelmed, confused, and likely not very excited. There are plenty of tutorials out there on how to properly edit. These tutorials have been created by professionals and will help you understand everything. They are available for all editing software.

Adobe Premiere Pro/Final Cut is my favorite software. But you can start with something simpler, such as iMovie. You will need to learn the basics of editing in no more than a week, according to me. This is a reasonable expectation. It becomes much easier from here to continue building up.

Google "how to do it" and you will find a lot of articles or YouTube videos explaining how to achieve the effect. The only thing that's required is a lot more practice and a few extra weeks of hard work. Once you start editing videos quickly, you will save a lot of time.

Video Thumbnails

Thumbnails are images that preview your video. It is the preview that people see before they click it. It could be a screenshot directly from your video, or it could be an image you created that does not contain any part of your video. Video thumbnails are vital to the success of your videos. They can grab people's attention as well as the title of your video. It is a good idea to take the time and learn how to make thumbnails of each of your videos.

Keep in mind, your goal is attract attention to the video. It is important to choose images of high quality that relate to what your video is about. Avoid using thumbnails that don't relate to the content of your video to gain views. It will not work long-term and frustrate your audience. Users click on the thumbnails to expect something but get something else. YouTube doesn't allow it. Instead, you should learn how create your own thumbnails for your videos.

Here's how.

Allow custom thumbnails first. Once you have verified your account, you can enable custom thumbnails. There are many ways that you can create your thumbnail. It really comes down to what works best. GIMP and Pixlr are just a few of the software options that you can use to accomplish this. Whatever makes it easier. Paint is also available if you are looking for something simpler. Once you have an image that fits your video, you can enrich it with text and/or images (optional).

If you would like a specific screenshot of your gameplay to appear as the thumbnail, you can do this another way. Tubebuddy.com/go provides a simple way to do this. It allows you to access the plugin on all browsers. Next you'll see a button that allows you to use a thumbnail generator to create a customized thumbnail for your video. Simply click on this plugin and select the frame that interests you. You can also choose your background color, as well as other options. You can explore the various features and have fun with it.

Once your Thumbnail is complete, it's time to upload it. Go to Video Manger, locate and click on the thumbnail that you would like to upload, then click on Edit. Click the Custom thumbnail link and upload the image. You are now ready to go.

Video Title

Your video title needs to give a short description of the content of your video. The thumbnail and the video title are what people will use to decide if your video is worth their time before clicking on it. It's important to have high-quality thumbnails. The same applies to your video title. This is basically a short line of text. The goal of the video title is to grab viewers' attention in a single sentence and make them click that play button. It only takes one line to convince people that your video is worthwhile and valuable.

Effective video titles are only possible if you understand what your target audience is looking for when they go to YouTube. Get out of your box and think about what your audience is most interested. This will help to name your video accurately and also provide you with new video ideas each time you do it. You can then think about the keywords people are searching. These keywords can be found using the Google Keyword Tool. It's easy to search for these keywords and find what you are looking for.

Once you've found the words that you feel are most relevant to your topic, choose the words you wish to include, and then create a compelling video title. Keep your video title between 14-15 words. YouTube's algorithms might find it suspicious if you go beyond that.

You should follow the guidelines, just as with the thumbnails. The algorithm can detect when you are over-saturating your videos in keywords. If this happens, it will stop ranking you high. This is because it will assume your videos have been spammed. You need to think like your target audience. The title should be structured in a way that your target audience is most likely search for what it wants on the platform.

Video Tags

Tags, another form of metadata help users find your YouTube video when they search for specific keywords. In order to rank your video high on the search engine, you should first tag it. Like hashtags in social media, they allow you to group similar content together. They aid the algorithm in determining whether your video is appropriate for the site and worth being displayed. Although tagging appears simple enough, there's a proper and wrong way. Let me tell you what I recommend for you to do when tagging your videos.

You'll notice several boxes appear when you upload your video. One for the video name, one each for the description and one for tags. A list of suggested tags can be found inside the tags panel. They may not always be relevant so you should disregard them.

YouTube has made them as a suggestion and they can be used to guide you.

I suggest you first include your particular keyword tags in this box. These are keywords that describe the main points of your video. If you are making a video about climbing the ladder at Solo Queue of League of Legends your keyword tags will likely look something along these lines: League of Legends. Solo Queue. Ranked. Elio climbing. These are the most relevant keywords to the video you are making. It is possible to sometimes look at other videos and copy some keywords. After you've entered a tag you will need to hit Enter.

After you are done with the keyword tags add some compound tags. These are short combinations or words that describe the entire video. These words should be kept short and simple. Think about your target audience and what they are likely to search on YouTube for.

That's all you need to properly tag your videos. Do not use tags that you know are highly searched, but don't have anything to do with your video content. YouTube algorithm will punish you for using them. Your video will not appear in search results and will be ranked lower on the search engine if people are looking for similar videos. YouTube's rules are important and you should not try to beat them.

Video Descriptions

YouTube's video descriptions can be used to identify whether your videos match the content you are searching for. These are short descriptions of your video's content. These descriptions are essential and should be included in all videos. A few boxes will appear each time you upload your video. One of them is called the description box. Here you will include your video description.

It should be short and simple. Do not make it long and complicated with irrelevant or unnecessary information. YouTube uses your video description to decide where it will show up. After your brief description of the video has been completed, you can add all the ways that people may interact with you.

This includes your email address (through which sponsors may contact you to arrange arrangements), all your social media connections, and your Patreon account where people can directly support your work by making small monthly payment. It is important that people are able to easily find ways to contact you. You can't tell whether people will click on the about page once they have seen your video. It is better not to be sorry. This is it. An easy formula for video descriptions that works everytime.

Connect with your Audience

Interacting in a meaningful way with your audience shows you care. Always reply to all comments on your videos. People have put in the effort to see your video and to leave comments. You owe them a response. While a simple "Thanks!" can work, I have found that responses that are between 2 and 3 lines work best. They show that you took the time to read their comment, and that you responded.

It is inevitable to get mean comments sometimes. Don't worry about it. As I said, it is important to be able differentiate between constructive criticism and hateful, internet-troll-ish comments. It's better not to reply defensively or try to reason with negativity.

If other people see that your hate responses are continuing, they will realize that you're vulnerable. This will make it easier for them to attack you and cause more problems in your comment section. Block the individual who keeps trolling your comments area multiple times. You won't lose a loyal customer, you just removed a troll from your comment section that was threatening your authority to your viewers.

YouTube comments can be used as a way to interact and respond with your followers. You can also do the same with your social media.

We'll be discussing your social strategy in Chapter 6. Once in a while, create questions and answer videos. This is where you answer all the most requested questions. All of these are a sign that you care for your followers and appreciate what they have said. Everybody likes being heard because it makes them feel valuable. It helps you to build a strong bond with your audience, which is vital if it's your goal to make a decent living. Use every opportunity to interact with your audience.

As your site grows at a rapid pace, you will find it becomes overwhelming and tedious to respond every comment. You won't be capable of keeping up with it all, but you should do your best. Once you reach this stage of growth simply reply to the most popular comments on videos.

You'd be surprised at how many people are emotionally attached to famous creators. Because the creator didn't make the effort to establish a strong relationship between people, this is why it's so common. It doesn't matter how much subscribers you have. It only matters how loyal followers your brand has attracted. These are your loyal followers who will follow and share your content with others, and even buy your products.

Get efficient and create your videos quickly in bulk

Videomaking can be very time-consuming. It's important to find ways to reduce the time it takes to create videos. You will be able to devote more time to your marketing efforts and promotions for your channel or products.

Each task that you perform has a set-up time. This includes the basics of operations such as putting down, getting distracted, gathering resources, starting the software, and getting focussed. The best time management tip for tasks that you are doing multiple times per week is to do them all in one sitting.

Instead of editing each day, edit all your week's footage in one go. Film your materials only once a week or on weekends if you are able to. This eliminates the set-up time necessary to begin each task. It also allows you get into the flow of things, which can make you more productive. This is how YouTube's top creators manage to spend their time.

You Would Like to Learn More about Growing Rapidly On YouTube?

These are some great tips. If you want to know more about YouTube, then you can read my book: Your Blueprient for Success. It will teach you how to increase your YouTube traffic and grow quickly. It covers everything you need for success on the platform. If you consider this important, then it is. It will pay off if your are willing to act and implement the techniques.

Chapter 8: How to Become an Effective Streamer

We talked about YouTube, the biggest video-sharing site, and how you have to be there if it is your dream. Twitch.tv stands for Twitch.tv among all streaming video platforms that live gameplay. The statistics are as impressive as the numbers: Twitch.tv boasts more than 110,000,000 views per month, close to 2 million unique broadcasters (which we will discuss later in this Chapter), and over 13000 Twitch Partners. It also has more peak concurrent viewers of over 2,000,000 across the side. These numbers are only going to rise.

But why are so many people drawn to watching other people play video games? People who have similar interests or are entertaining and skilled enjoy it. You have probably seen the streaming streams on the site. It's all about how you experience the stream. The question is: How can you get started as an streamer? And how can you achieve success on Twitch.tv.

Streaming Equipment

Let's discuss the steps you will need to get started. Go to Twitch.tv to create an account. It's free and fast. Fill in all required details.

Next, choose which platform you want to stream. For each of these, you will need an internet link that can stream at high resolution (720p – 1080p). This will allow you to upload 5 MB/sec. It is possible to get 3-3.5MB upload speed but I recommend that you keep it at a minimum of 5MB. Choose a cable internet connection over wireless. Cable is faster, and it's more stable. If you plan to stream on a PlayStation 4, you will need a DualShock 4 controller, a PS4 console, and the game you are streaming. The Xbox controller, Xbox console and the video you are streaming on Xbox are required.

Minimum hardware requirements are required for PCs. These requirements are dependent on the game you want to play. In any event, it's important to invest in hardware that is going to perform well and will last you longer. I recommend you have at the very least 4GB RAM, a decent graphics cards (Nvidia GeForce GTX970 is my favorite, though it isn't necessarily the most cost-effective) and a powerful processor (latest Core i7).

In order to get the best performance, it is important that each component of your equipment works together. It is possible to stream League of Legends on hardware with less specs than the ones listed above. If you want to stream a more resource-intensive title, your hardware must be even more powerful.

You will also need a decent quality video camera (I'll show you why later) along with a pair of headphones. I would not spend large sums on a high end keyboard or mouse. I haven't found any added advantages to high-end gear, so pick something that is easy on the wrists and feels comfortable. Get a high-quality microphone. Make sure that the audio is clear. The Zalman ZMMIC1 and Blue

Snowball are my favorites. Or, if your preference is for something more extreme, the Blue Yeti.

You will need software to broadcast the gameplay. OBS or XSplit would be the two most used and I recommend them. I won't bore with the stats on which one you prefer. Don't get distracted by the minute details. Both of them can be used for free and will get the job done. You don't need to worry about the small details.

You can stream by simply installing the program that you like and creating an account. You can then launch the program again. After logging in, the program will be able to access your live stream. Use the settings menu to customize the audio and visual options that best suit your needs. Don't be discouraged if they aren't perfected the first time. Over time, as your audience gives feedback, you will see exactly what they want.

Even if you don't have the money, don't try to purchase the most expensive hardware. While your viewers deserve the best, make sure you only spend what you can afford. From there, you can build up. You can always increase the number of products or services you offer once you are making profits.

Set up your streaming schedule and be consistent

In Chapter 1, I explained how important it was for you to have a plan that you can stick to and manage. A streaming schedule on Twitch.tv can be even more important than on YouTube. This is because anyone can access your YouTube videos at any time during the week as long as they are uploaded consistently. This is why posting on Monday, Wednesday, or Friday at 8pm is not an absolute requirement. However, it can be helpful for SEO.

Twitch.tv offers a unique way to broadcast live gameplay. If they don't know ahead of time when you will stream, it is likely they will miss it. You can rely on more than the follow button.

People will quickly forget about your stream if you are absent from it for too many times. Not only that, but scheduling allows new viewers who have just found your stream to find out when they can catch you up again.

Due to the huge amount of people streaming popular games, you must be able stream weekly if your goal is to make it. Stream at the identical hours every week. The more stream you do, the better. Every day is best. If you have hundreds upon thousands of followers and are busy managing many things, such as speaking opportunities, sponsorship obligations, managing employee relations, or additional marketing campaigns, you may not be able to stream every week. Because you would have built up your loyal following through months and years worth of hard work. From this point on, it is just a matter sustaining what you have. Your reach will continue scaling organically.

But if this is your first time streaming, it's okay to skip the weekly thing. Streaming should be done as often, and for as long you are able to do so. I recommend streaming 4x a week for 8hrs. But every day is best. Let's not forget that we are talking about you stacking shelves and playing games. If you're reading this book, this is probably something you would do. Part-time working is not going to lead you to full-time success. This isn't a scheme to make it rich fast. The point is that streaming and YouTube must be a priority for you if your goal is to achieve the financial freedom and lifestyle that you want by playing video games.

Do your best to squeeze in as much streaming time as you can, even if your schedule is full of school, work, friends and family. If you decide you can only stream 30 hours per day, stream more for less time. It's better to stream six days per week for five hours than three days for ten hours. Streaming regularly will help you get more exposure. People often browse between broadcasters to check out new streams.

Stream at peak times, when the viewer counts are highest, and always. While it will take some research to identify trends and tendencies in your game, you should do so once you have. The ideal scenario would have you streaming at the peak time of viewership, even though most of the streamers for that particular game are offline. I've found that people get bored waiting for their streamer to arrive online. They are therefore more willing to give smaller streams a shot to fill the gap. It's possible to make a good impression and try to get people hooked so that they return again the next morning.

How to be a Twitch partner

Important thing to know is that your stream must focus on your AUDIENCE. Not about you. Yes, that's right. That's it. Repeat it for as long and often as you need to remember. Let's return to the reason so many people see gaming streams. Ask someone who hasn't experienced the streaming scene how millions upon millions of people prefer to see others play videogames and they will not be able to answer your question.

It's all down to the enjoyment they get from it - both the social, and the emotional. Imagine sitting down with a friend to watch a streamer. Your personality is crucial as a streamer. This is because it attracts people to you without you having to be the best at the particular game you are playing (although being good won't hurt). Trust me, regardless of how great you are, someone will always be faster than your buttons and better at the game. Your personality is all that is unique about your stream. Your ability communicate your thoughts, feelings and emotions to lift others' morale, make people laugh, and relate is something that's unique to you.

A lot of games can be stressful because they are competitive. It's easy get burned out trying to climb up the League of Legends ranks. Oh, and by the way, if you are interested in that topic, there is a book I wrote called 30 days to Diamond. You can find it also on Kindle. It has helped hundreds of people, and I just love the feedback it's received.

But I digress. Some people enjoy being able to watch the progress of the game from their perspective, while others prefer to do the same thing. It's lots of fun. You can learn from other players' strategies and their approach to a problem you may have run into. It's a great place to communicate with your community and watch their reactions on twitch.

I am telling you this because once your stream is focused on your audience, you will find it easy to partner with Twitch.tv.

Let me explain. Look at the minimum requirements that you must meet to be eligible to become a Twitch Partner. It's not an easy task. These are the 3 requirements.

-500 viewers concurrently per stream

Stream at the minimum three times per week, every week

-Your contents must conform to their Terms of Service, and DMCA Guidelines.

You can see that there is only one requirement that is hard to meet: the 500 concurrent users. It's only a guideline. Each case can be handled individually. It's actually much easier than this. I've known people who got partnered while receiving only 50 concurrent viewers. Because their streams were always about their viewers, that is why they did it. The streamers were attentive to every comment made in Twitch chat and interacted in all possible ways with their audience. They demonstrated their commitment and consistency by streaming every morning. They will be able to see the potential you stream has and will favor you for the program.

Again, viewership is irrelevant. There is no magic number. If you have 500 followers on trolls but are not interested in interacting with them, chances are that your application will be denied. You should first focus on frequency and consistency before you think about applying. If you do this you will quickly get your Twitch partner within weeks. Provided you get at most 50 people streaming at the times you stream, and that you stream every day at the same times, it is possible to earn your Twitch sponsorship.

How to Be an Expert in Audience Interaction

We already know the reasons why people view streams. The main reason people watch streams is to have a conversation with someone they can trust, who can entertain and make their day more enjoyable. It is why you need to get a Webcam. So people can SEE YOU! The first thing to do is set up a webcam. The webcam will let people see you and make it easier to communicate with them.

People feel more at home if they are able to see your face as you play. After they become used to it, they will feel that they know you. Plus, they can see your reactions. This makes your personality more credible as you can't hide your body language and natural expressions.

This is a downside because people may pick up on clues that your personality might be fake. You might be behaving artificially to please your donors and get them to make a donation. Your body language will show it. Now, I get it. Maybe you don't want to use a websitecam because you are insecure or afraid that others might not like you. Or maybe you feel uncomfortable having people stare at you while you play.

Let it go. If you intend to become famous, people will talk all about you. No matter how conscious you may be, they will share images and information about yourself. Regardless what you do to avoid being bullied verbally, 5%-10% people will talk about and bully you verbally. Your envy is your problem, not theirs.

It's almost impossible to have insecurities beyond your head. It is human nature. Most people don't care much about your flaws. They love you for what you are. These people will be your loyal supporters and the only ones you should actually care about. Confidence is gained by showing vulnerability even when you aren't feeling comfortable.

People will feel they know you when you are on camera. It's a way of saying that if they watch your stream every morning, they will start to consider you a friend. Make them feel important. If they answer your questions, call them by their first name. For taking the time and effort to comment, thank them. Encourage them further to take action. Ask them to contact you offline and tell them that you're available to help.

You can play songs on stream to them if you have a good question, or if there is a lot of chat comment activity.

Make sure to relate to your audience in all possible ways. When you receive a question from someone going through difficult times, say so. People love being understood. Let them know about your experience, how it went for you, and what you did afterwards. Then, share the good side. Being a human being and listening to their stories is a great way to show that you care.

You'll be amazed at how much your audience responds to you if they take the time to cheer you up. Sometimes streaming can be difficult. You can make YOUR day better if your audience has a good connection. It's an all-win-win situation. It's astonishing how this works. It's the principle reciprocity put into action. It's the way human relations work.

Always respond to donations. Imagine this, people might pay money for you to say "Thanks so much for making my day easier" or ask you a question. It's because they respect you enough and feel connected with you. If you ignore the message, as long it's not something bad, they will be able to stop you from doing it again. Refusing to respond to donation messages can cost you your money. Always show your appreciation for their support. These are the things you should do if people care enough about your well-being to give you hard-earned money.

Talk, talk, talk. All you have to do is speak while you stream. But what about speaking about? Anything positive, relevant and uplifting. Tell a joke you just learned. Tell them about a fun story you've been part of. Tell them about your childhood. Your good and bad moments. What are your values? And what do you hope to achieve in life. Anything that has positive meaning. This allows others to get to to know you and builds trust.

This is the kinda stuff that will grow you as a streamer. When you do these things, people will begin talking about your stream on their social media. This is where a lot more of your viewership is going to come. You'll notice that your stream is flooded with new viewers, all the while waiting for their experience. It's an extremely rewarding way to bring in organic viewer traffic.

How to Make Your Stream More Enjoyable

Optimizing your stream is essential if you want viewers to enjoy it. The music you listen to is just one aspect of optimizing your stream. Spotify or Rdio subscriptions allow you to play your favourite music without issues. Keep in mind that bad songs can quickly turn people from your stream. It is important to choose songs that people enjoy. What I have discovered is that people prefer a more relaxed stream environment and relaxing music to heavy metal. These are just anecdotal observations.

You can ensure that people have a better experience by what they talk about. I mentioned in a previous paragraph that it's better to talk more often than not, so long as there is no silence. Be positive and only discuss things that bring joy. Avoid talking about negative topics. People don't want to hear about your problems because there are likely many.

Why should they bother with another's difficulties? People need to find a way out of their own troubles and if your stream is not providing that, they'll switch to your competitor. Talking negatively about things is a way to channel negative energy. This can easily cause tension and can result in viewers becoming more anxious. Talk about things you can lift and entertain your viewers. Avoid gossip, which can quickly become boring and make you look bad.

Next, make sure you invest in high-quality custom channel art. This banner is what represents the visual elements of your stream. This banner helps you to attract viewers' attention, and can boost your credibility. Adobe Photoshop makes it easy to create amazing banners. You can always outsource this task if your skills are not up to the mark or you simply don't have the time.

A graphic designer, or someone on fiverr.com, can create beautiful and unique channel artwork in return for a modest amount of money. A fiverr.com graphic designer will charge you about $5. You can also use them for offline screen images, which you can then import into your broadcasting programs. The offline screen photo is a great idea. It allows you to add information about the schedule, so that people who have seen you stream live after your session has ended, will know when it's available.

Get cool subscription and donation notifications. These are in-stream alerts that will appear whenever someone subscribes, donates, or donates to your channel. It's a good idea if you have one alert for donations, and another for subscriptions. For your viewers, nothing is more rewarding than seeing a personalized alert pop up in stream due to them subscribing or donating money.

It could be funny sound effects accompanied by a message. This helps to create a relaxing and enjoyable atmosphere. You can also set donations goals for certain amounts (such as funding a new laptop) and other features. To create these, go to www.twitchalerts.com. Look at the things that interest you.

While we are on the subject of visual art, you can create unique and original subscriber-only messages. These are custom images that your subscribers will receive when they subscribe to your channel. From my experience, sub-emotes have been a great way to get people to subscribe. These sub-emotes can be used throughout Twitch.tv and on any Twitch channel. You can create sub emotes by using Gimp or Photoshop. Or you can hire someone to create them. You can have more sub-emotes if you have more subscribers. In the beginning, there are 2 subscribers. Then they increase in number as shown below.

10 Subs = +2 (4 total)

50 Subs = +2 (6 total)

100 Subs = +2 (8 total)

250 Subs = +2 (10 total)

500 Subs = +5 (15 total)

1000 Subs = +5 (20 total)

2000 Subs = +5 (25 total)

3000 Subs = +5 (30 total)

4000 Subs = +5 (35 total)

5000 Subs = +5 (40 total)

6000 Subs = +5 (45 total)

7000 Subs = +5 (50 total)

Keep your Twitch Chat Clean

Let's not be naive. Twitch chats can be quite chaotic and overwhelming at times. Some people use the platform to vent frustration, such as trolling or toxicity towards other streamers. Botted accounts can also be found in chat rooms to send spam and viruses. It's a big deterrent. Even if they love your stream they will soon leave if they see spam and trolls. The more popular the games you play, the more you will get trolled.

Chat bots are a great way to manage everything. You can even create your chat bot via mIRC. Install the program. Create another Twitch user account to link it to the bot. Once that is done, use the program's customizable settings to customize your experience. I would also recommend that you hire chat moderators to keep an eye on chats and make sure they meet your standards. They can remove offensive posts and troll discussion. It is important to appoint people you like and who are regular viewers of your stream. So that you get the most from your stream, make sure to be very specific.

Stop allowing a single user to post continuously negative comments. Twitch chat is intended to encourage interaction between users and help them build a community. If they aren't interested in being a good user on your channel and just want to ruin the experience for everyone, they won't be welcome. You should not allow them to ruin someone else's job. Trolls can be thought of as weeds in an attractive garden. Keep your garden clean and free of weeds. The flowers will become more beautiful. If you allow the weeds to grow, that's all you get.

Join forces with streamers that you like

Are you a friend of a streamer with a similar audience? Ask them if you can collaborate. It could be something you can host together, or simply the opportunity to play the same game. They will generally accept your proposal if they feel you have managed your channel well. Everyone wants to be associated, at least in part, with people who are well received and respected in their respective communities. It's a win/win situation as both you and your audience are exposed for free.

Before you approach someone to collaborate with, it is important to think honestly about the benefits they will get from it. If you are just beginning your stream and have 10 concurrent viewers, and your streamer has over 500, how much do you gain from that collaboration?

Try to view things from their perspective. Consider yourself their perspective. My advice is to put your entire focus on audience building when you're first starting out. Once you have about 50-100 simultaneous viewers consistently, you can think about reaching out to other streamers and offering them collabs. You will not receive any responses if they are the same size as you.

You can even host streamers you like after you finish streaming. This allows you to direct your viewers towards the person you hosted. If other streamers are of the same size as you, and you're willing to host streams and promote others' streams, they'll often host yours in the hopes that you return the favor. You've just gained viewers. And if they do so, it's basically sharing traffic. It is a win-win scenario.

Celebrate Your Sub Button

Being partnered for your first time is a feeling that I could only compare with getting your first good grade in school or your first great job. It is like you are at the top of the universe and nothing can stop your success. You should celebrate when you receive your Sub Button. It will show them you care and reward them for their support.

You can give away some kind of giveaway. You can either sing a song for a reward or have a small contest that you keep secret. It's a great way to show people you care about Twitch.tv.

You can get good at the sport you are playing

Let me be clear. For success, it is not necessary to be the best at what you stream. People don't care that much about how well you do. They don't care about how good you are. What matters is whether they have a happy experience and what makes them feel more positive about their day. It doesn't matter if the game is new to you or if it is just plain awful. You should invest some time in learning. Aim to reach an acceptable level of performance that won't embarrass yourself in front your viewers.

If you are a proficient player, you will definitely have an advantage over the rest. Being a streamer doesn't mean you have to be the best. However, being decent is enough. Ensure your stream provides some educational value. People can learn a lot from your stream. It might be an in game strategy or simply knowledge. Do not limit your entertainment to telling jokes all day.

Get to Know Your Audience

It is the best way to distinguish yourself from other streamers, to really get to know your audience. Listen to what they have on certain topics. Do not discuss controversial topics, such as religion or racism. Ask them questions to help you understand their comments. Ask them what they do for fun. Initiate interesting conversations.

Talk about your common interests with your gaming community. As much as you can, get to know them. This will allow you to be different from 95% if your competitors, most of whom never think about it. This is especially true when you are just starting but you will need to continue applying it as you increase your experience. It will take some effort and extra time but you will see the benefits in the long-term.

These are the key elements that will make a real difference and keep people coming back.

Make it easy and simple for others to find your Stream

Get active on your social networks. Post at minimum 3 times per hour, every day. Your stream will be linked on all your social networks, including YouTube. Make sure you post new content every time your stream is live, so that others who are using Social media can also see it. It is important to post content that requires engagement from readers. Next

Chapter: I'll be discussing how to market and promote your content.

Use provocative stream titles. To grab people's attention, you only have one line. Make sure to update it regularly and include any exciting work you do. It is important to mention that you are doing an unranked, 24-hour challenge (League of Legends). It is important to describe the stream in a way that people will be interested without making it seem needy. Do not TELL people why they should be watching your stream. People don't like being told what you should do. Simply use stream titles to show them you value their opinion.

A game that's well-known and well-followed is a good choice. This would include League of Legends, Counter-Strike Global Offensive and Fallout 4. HearthStone Heroes of Warcraft is another popular title. Streaming a popular title will increase your exposure and allow you to network with other streamers.

Your stream and YouTube videos will only reach a certain number of people if a game is popular enough. If you are unable to make a living with a game with just 100 viewers across Twitch.tv you won't be able play it. There are many games that you can play and you can test them once you have thousands. However, it's not feasible to become a millionaire if you don't watch what is most popular.

Chapter 9: How to market and promote your content

This Chapter is by far my favorite. It's my favorite Chapter because it feels like it's going the most to help you. It's a skill that is essential if you want reach your target audience today.

I've noticed that people don't always enjoy the marketing part of creating your brand. You're creative and like to create content. However, it's essential that people find your content. Or, simply direct people to your content.

Recall that more than 500 hours worth of video are uploaded to YouTube each minute, as mentioned in previous Chapters. Twitch is being streamed by thousands right now. It has never made it easier to be discovered as a content maker than it is today, and it will get more difficult over time.

It is essential to be equally adept at marketing and content creation. It's just how it is and will continue to be. Let me emphasize it once more: How well you communicate your brand to others is an important factor in how successful you will be at making a career from video games.

In this Chapter, I will be listing 24 effective ways you can promote your content. All of them yield results. They work when you are just starting, as well as as you continue to grow. They work well for your blog as well YouTube videos, products, and Twitch streams. Let's begin.

1: Your Social Media Strategy

Social media is THE modern way to reach people with an internet connection. This is why it is essential for your brand to use social media. How can you promote social media content without feeling overwhelmed? If you've ever tried to participate on every platform, you know how tiring and time-consuming it can become. Here are the key points to keep in mind as you promote your content through social media.

First, choose the platforms that interest you. Your goal is to not use as many platforms possible. It will not lead to any success if you disperse all your efforts. You will never be committed to the platforms that you use if this is your goal. People will quickly notice that you do not want to interact. The key to success on social media is being able and willing to interact with your audience, and if possible, building a relationship. With social media, you should use fewer platforms.

Social media marketing has the 80/20 principle. It is a rule that 80 percent of your marketing efforts should come from 20 per cent of the social networks you use. It is recommended that you promote your brand with 20% of your posts, while 80% should be posted to content that appeals to your target audience.

Do not try to be all things to everyone on Linked in. Stick to Facebook, Instagram, Twitter and Facebook. Pinterest is an option if your content focuses primarily on visuals.

That's it. These should be your first priority when you think about social media. Limit your attention to them because they will bring you the greatest results.

Consistency in social media is crucial. You need to be consistent about following people (so you can follow them back) on daily basis, building relationships and posting regularly things that interest your target audience. Do it again and again. It's all about the time. You will not see much improvement if the consistency you show for one week is consistent. Your path will take you down the right road if it is followed for several months. If you stick to your strategy for years you will experience exponential growth.

It is essential to understand the viewpoint of your ideal target audience in order to make posts that generate results. You can ask them what they'd like to see. Ask yourself why you target audience uses social networks in the first instance. Does it allow them to make new friends, learn new things and interact with people who have similar interests as theirs? What is their likely age? How about their gender? This information can help you determine the content that you should post to social media.

There are tools that you can utilize to greatly improve your social media efforts. You will find the one that works best for you. They are both free and easy to use, which will help you save a lot of time. Buffer is my favorite. You can use it to schedule up ten posts (that's free) in a queue. It works for Twitter and Facebook as well as LinkedIn, Pinterest, and LinkedIn.

This is great if you know you will not be in town over the weekend but need to keep your twitter activity up. You can set up your posts to be posted every 6 hours so your viewers don't miss any of your updates. Hootsuite is another option for scheduling. Mention.com, a social media monitoring tool, can help you monitor mentions in social media. These are all fantastic ways to optimize your time marketing on social media.

Make sure to update your followers regularly with news about your brand. Anything that may interest your fans. Post about any giveaways you're planning to run or the charity streams you intend to support. Linking to your blog posts is a great way to get more traffic to you website. It also gives you more SEO advantages due to the backlinks to your site from social networks. Each post should include a call out to action. Encourage people to subscribe and follow your YouTube channel.

2: Forums

Forums are meant to facilitate information sharing about common interests. There are forums that cover almost any topic. The purpose of these forums is to provide useful information and help others. There are many gaming communities for popular games in every language. It's your task to find the 2 most active gaming forums for the stream you are watching and become a member.

Limit yourself to two. It's too time-consuming. Forums don't allow you to just create an account and upload your YouTube and stream videos and expect thousands of people will check them out. People will ignore your posts if this is the case. They will conclude that you are a desperate marketer who spams forums in order to promote their own products and offer no value for members.

Promoting content through forums can be done in a way that adds value to the community. Join the conversation. Post interesting material in the different threads. You can vote for other people's posts if they make something of value. Join the chat room and add friends. Long, detailed, and well thought out posts should be written about all aspects of the game.

As long you continue to provide value, people will eventually find an interest and start to look at your profile more often to see any new activity. Your profile is where you'll find all of your Twitch streams and YouTube channels. This is where you will get the best results from forums.